"Most business books these days either rehash the same themes or merely validate what you already know. It's refreshing to read *Power Branding* and be able to apply so many things both your customers and marketing team will appreciate."

—*Jay Steinfeld, CEO/Founder, Blinds.com*

"Any business, regardless of size or scope, will gain a lifetime of practical value from the lessons in *Power Branding*."

—*John Jantsch, author of* Duct Tape Marketing

"Steve draws on his deep, real-world experience to show precisely why (and how) you can transform your brand from '*meh*' to '*Holy Cow*'. If you want your product or service to truly stand out in a crowded marketplace, buy this book. (If you don't, buy it anyway—Steve will convince you why you're wrong by the end of chapter three.)"

—*Les McKeown,* Wall Street Journal *and* USA Today
bestselling author of Predictable Success: Getting Your
Organization On the Growth Track—and Keeping It There
and The Synergist: How to Lead Your Team to Predictable Success

"Steve McKee is a marketer's personal trainer, and *Power Branding* is a great workout for any plan. Tons of practical ways to shake the dust off any brand. Every marketer . . . scratch that, every business person needs to read *Power Branding*. This is not one that will sit on the shelf—you'll dog-ear the heck out of it and find yourself creating your new plan with each power-packed chapter."

—*Steve Born, VP, Marketing, Globus Family of Brands*

"As stewards of strong brands, we have a fundamental obligation to nurture and support our greatest asset. *Power Branding* seamlessly weaves together the most important and relevant concepts to this end in an enjoyable, easy-to-read manner that will be required reading for our entire marketing and sales team."

—*Todd Talbot, President of Fluidmaster, Inc.*

"Building on his insightful work in BusinessWeek.com and *When Growth Stalls*, Steve does an amazing job of making the potential of 'Power Branding' accessible to us all."

—*Michael Brenner, blogger, speaker and VP of
Marketing and Content Strategy at SAP*

"Steve worked with our brand to help us very successfully find our brand voice. This book is filled with many of the strategies he used. It's a common sense, how-to book that CEOs and business leaders who want to grow their brands should read."

—*Mary Kennedy Thompson, President, Mr. Rooter Plumbing*

"*Power Branding* is a unique journey into the heart and soul of a brand. I plan to use this book as a brainstorming tool with my organization, which is working hard to make our century-plus old brand more relevant in today's marketplace. This is a great read for you and your company!"

—*Mark Korros, CEO, Pendleton Woolen Mills*

"Great arguments, great organization, great examples! *Power Branding* works so well as a book because it cuts right to the heart of what it means to be a brand in the digital age. This book is a must-read for any professional hoping to keep up in the era of the social business!"

—*Cheryl Burgess, author of* The Social Employee, *and CEO, Blue Focus Marketing*

"Another book on branding? No. This is not just another book on branding. Steve McKee walks readers through the *who, what, how, where and when* to help business leaders and marketers get their brand on track. He even includes the "whoops" so we can learn from others' mistakes. This is an important read full of practical examples for businesses small and large."

—*Lisa Gerber, Big Leap Creative*

"*Power Branding* helps you cut through information overload and use audience, strategy, creativity, and execution to build a brand . . . a long-lasting brand that withstands the perils of instant gratification and the shiny, new penny."

—*Gini Dietrich, founder and CEO of Arment Dietrich, co-author of* Marketing and the Round, *and author of* Spin Sucks

"*Power Branding* is valuable because Steve covers all the good practices great companies visibly use to be successful. *Power Branding* is a must-read because it reveals so many shrewd concepts that are not obvious."

—*Al Pepi, Alonti Catering and Alonti Cafes*

"*Power Branding* brings relevance to evergreen branding principles which every company needs. Definitely a resource to keep around when you have to make some tough decisions about your brand."

—*Cody Vance Pierce, Vice President of Marketing, Pizza Ranch*

POWER BRANDING

LEVERAGING THE SUCCESS OF THE WORLD'S BEST BRANDS

STEVE McKEE

palgrave
macmillan

POWER BRANDING
Copyright © Steve McKee, 2014.
All rights reserved.

First published in 2014 by PALGRAVE MACMILLAN® in the United
States—a division of St. Martin's Press LLC, 175 Fifth Avenue, New York,
NY 10010.

Where this book is distributed in the UK, Europe and the rest of the
world, this is by Palgrave Macmillan, a division of Macmillan Publishers
Limited, registered in England, company number 785998, of Houndmills,
Basingstoke, Hampshire RG21 6XS.

Palgrave Macmillan is the global academic imprint of the above companies
and has companies and representatives throughout the world.

Palgrave® and Macmillan® are registered trademarks in the United States,
the United Kingdom, Europe and other countries.

ISBN 978-1-137-27884-5

Library of Congress Cataloging-in-Publication Data

McKee, Steve, 1963-
    Power branding : leveraging the success of the world's best brands / by
Steve McKee.
      pages   cm
    ISBN 978-1-137-27884-5 (alk. paper)
    1. Branding (Marketing) 2. Brand name products. I. Title.
HF5415.1255.M42   2014
658.8'27—dc23

                                                                2013024732

A catalogue record of the book is available from the British Library.

Design by Letra Libre

First edition: January 2014

10 9 8 7 6 5 4 3 2 1

Printed in the United States of America.

CONTENTS

HOW

WHERE AND WHEN

WHOOPS

To the six—

Denise, Delaney & Brandon, Riley, Cassidy and Garvey—

for whom I live and breathe

ACKNOWLEDGMENTS

IN SOME WAYS THIS BOOK HAS BEEN A DECADE IN THE MAKING, as it was ten years ago that I began expressing my often-unconventional marketing and branding opinions at Businessweek.com. Thus, first thanks must go to Nick Leiber and the team at Bloomberg Businessweek for letting me work out my branding philosophy a thousand words at a time (and to James Korenchen for making the original introduction way back when).

In another sense this book has taken a career to write. It's difficult to acknowledge all of the great thinkers who have informed my long-studied understanding of business in general and branding in particular. David Ogilvy, Jack Trout, Al Ries, Lisa Fortini-Campbell, Michael Porter, Malcolm Gladwell, Thomas Sowell, Ted Levitt, Chris Zook, and many more opened my eyes to first principles and have guided my thoughts as I have worked my way through the rough-and-tumble, Wild West world in which I've made my living.

Ultimately, however, this book is a lifetime in the making, and I would be remiss not to thank the authors I first discovered as a teen—Moses, David, Peter, Paul, and, of course, Matthew, Mark, Luke, and John—writers of old who, guided by the Holy Spirit, gave me an understanding of the nature of man and the predicament we're in as we await our ultimate redemption. That understanding is, in my view, essential in coming to a full-orbed appreciation of why people buy and sell and tussle and trade, act sometimes rationally and other times irrationally, and allow their thoughts in some cases and feelings in others to drive their purchase decisions. It is my humble hope that this book can be of help to those who want to do the best they can with what they've got as we all muddle our way through the fallen world in which we live.

Special thanks go to my patient-as-a-saint agent, Judith Ehrlich, and her colleague Sophia Seidner, who helped me shape and form and edit and proof the manuscript, and to Karen Wolny, Lauren LoPinto, and the rest of the team at Palgrave Macmillan for believing in this project.

I owe tremendous gratitude to the wonderful clients I've worked with throughout my career, who together have helped me learn (sometimes the hard way) a wide variety of real-world lessons, along with Pat Wallwork and the team at McKee Wallwork & Company, whose wisdom and work continues to amaze me. Finally, my thanks go to my loving God, my lovely wife, and my wonderful children, without whom none of this would be worthwhile.

INTRODUCTION

THE LAST TIME I WENT SHOPPING FOR A TELEVISION WAS BOTH confusing and enlightening. And a little bit embarrassing.

If you don't often stroll the aisles of your local electronics superstore, the experience can be somewhat overwhelming. After I found my way through the giant warehouse to the home entertainment section (no mean feat), I was confronted with literally dozens of televisions, all beaming and blaring as if they were clamoring for my attention: "Buy me!" "Buy me!" It was instant sensory overload.

I knew what size TV I wanted but was still left with a couple of dozen to sort through. My next step was to do what most rational consumers do when confronted with too much choice—I developed a shortcut.

I couldn't easily tell all of the different models apart so I simply ruled out the higher-priced options (why pay a premium?) and eliminated the lower-priced options (too cheap is risky), which narrowed my selection down to four or five. Ruling out a few more for picture quality reduced my choice to the beauty of the binary: this TV or that TV. So far, so good.

This is where I got stuck. I gazed at one TV, then the other, then back to the first again, stroking my chin like some amateur Einstein, for an absurdly long time. With the differences so negligible, I honestly didn't know which TV to choose and had a sneaking suspicion that the employees on break in the back were getting a good laugh watching me through the security camera.

It was then that I noticed something that, in an instant, made my decision simple. One TV was branded Dynex and one Toshiba.

Before I get to the punchline, which one do you think I bought?

I've used this illustration several times and I've never had anyone say anything other than Toshiba. And yes, that is the correct answer. I bought the television that was built by a brand that I both knew and respected. All other things being equal, Toshiba got my business because the brand has been around for some time and has earned a good reputation. Dynex was unfamiliar to me and therefore had built no reservoir of trust or equity in my mind. Case closed. Sale made.

This story is but one illustration of the raison d'être of this book: Of all the assets any company owns, its brand is the single most valuable. A bold statement? Sure. But think about it: A brand is the only corporate asset that, managed properly, will never depreciate. *Never depreciate.* Those are magic words. Patents expire, software ages, buildings crumble, roofs leak, machines break, and trucks wear out. But a well-managed brand can increase in value year after year after year. That's jaw-dropping.

In an exhaustive annual study on brand value conducted by Interbrand, a leading global branding consultancy, Coca-Cola has perennially been at or near the top of the list with a value of more than $75 billion. That's the value of the brand alone—not the bottling plants, the inventory, the truck fleets, the factories, the secret recipe—just the brand. According to the same study, the McDonald's brand is worth more than $40 billion, and the Toyota, BMW, and Mercedes brands all hover around $30 billion each.

Business-to-business (B2B) brands are no slouches either. IBM, the most valuable B2B brand in the world according to Interbrand, is worth almost as much as Coca-Cola at just over $74 billion. Other B2B brands among the top 20 include GE, Intel, Cisco, and Oracle. In fact, some 20 percent of the top 100 brands in Interbrand's study are primarily or exclusively B2B.[1]

Global research firm Millward Brown does its own annual brand valuation study with a different, though equally comprehensive, methodology.[2] Its "BrandZ" rankings are dissimilar only in degree, not in kind—similarly valuing Coca-Cola at around $75 billion but suggesting that the Google, IBM, and Apple brands are worth well over $100 billion each.[3] You can argue with the amounts but not with the premise:

The world's best brands, separate and distinct from their other corporate assets, are worth billions.

If that's the case, why is branding taken so lightly in the boardroom? I believe it's because it's misunderstood. Branding seems soft and fuzzy. It's often incorrectly defined. And (at least historically) it hasn't been a hard, measurable internal metric like sales, market share, stock price, or price/earnings ratio that a CFO can track on a spreadsheet or a CEO report to the board.

That being said, neglecting a brand is both naive and shortsighted for any company. Not only is nothing more potentially valuable, nothing is more important. In some ways branding is a victim of semantics; call it "reputation," and nobody in the C-suite would ever argue that it's anything less than critical.

Corporations are careful to avoid doing anything that would harm their reputations, intuitively understanding Will Rogers' quip: "It takes a lifetime to build a good reputation, but you can lose it in a minute."[4] (See "Bernie Madoff" or "BP.") But management teams commonly underachieve in the application of reputation management best practices—in a word, branding.

True effectiveness in branding requires a proper understanding of the concept. There isn't anything within an organization that a well-defined brand identity doesn't impact (and vice-versa). *Forbes* magazine, in partnership with the Reputation Institute, surveyed more than 55,000 consumers in 15 countries and asked them to describe their perceptions of the most highly regarded companies in the world. The study identified seven factors that drive corporate reputation: products and services (naturally), innovation, workplace, governance, citizenship, leadership, and performance.[5] There's very little that any company does that doesn't fall within one of those categories, something the best brands understand. (FedEx is now even tying performance review criteria to attributes defined by its brand platform.)

Effective branding improves the visibility of and respect for a product, service, or company and drives sales. It also enhances margins, as customers are willing to pay more for products and services from companies they know and trust. Branding can also improve the internal dynamics of an organization and impact both recruiting and employee turnover. And research now demonstrates that branding even affects financial metrics.

According to CoreBrand, a consultancy that has tracked more than 1,200 companies in 47 industries for more than two decades, the average positive impact of the brand on a public company's stock performance is 5 to 7 percent and in some cases significantly more.[6] And Britain's Bestra Brand Consultants analyzed nearly 500 of the largest U.K. and U.S. public corporations over a five-year period and developed an empirical model that used advanced regression analysis to test variables that might explain variations in market capitalization. According to the model, a 5 percent improvement in the strength of a corporation's reputation will lead to an increase of as much as 2 percent in its market cap.[7]

How would your world be different if your stock price was 5, 10, or 15 percent higher, or if the value of your company increased by 2 percent? This kind of impact can translate to immense wealth.

Branding is anything but lightweight, but too few companies intentionally manage their brands as the valuable corporate assets they are. Sure, all organizations do their best to be honest, to offer high-quality products, to provide responsive service, and to do whatever else will enhance their reputation, knowing that the way they do business affects the value of their company. But not all understand that the way they manage their brands can significantly impact the value of their business.

Here's how Larry Williams, Vice President for Marketing at Caterpillar (a B2B brand worth more than $6 billion according to Interbrand), put it: "We can influence people's decisions by shaping attitudes and perceptions. We can do this by building better products—and providing superior service. But we can also affect attitudes by managing the way we present ourselves. We are a different Caterpillar . . . we know it. But it's time to let the rest of the world in on the news."[8]

Indeed. And it's time to let the rest of the world in on the principles of *Power Branding*. The stakes are as high as the statistics are striking: 100 percent of marketing plans promise to generate growth, yet over the course of an average decade (to say nothing of recent years), more than half of all companies witness a decline in revenue for at least one year (and sometimes multiple years). The problem isn't a lack of desire or ambition—it's a lack of perspective, understanding, and insight.

Most busy businesspeople don't have time or inclination to study the ins and outs and ups and downs the world's master brands have discovered through trial and error. But over the course of a career as a marketing strategist that has spanned nearly 30 years, I have. And I hope to show you how you can leverage your most valuable asset by exploring notable brands' marketing strategies and explaining why they worked—or didn't.

Many of the principles in *Power Branding* I first expounded upon in my long-running column for Businessweek.com. Others arose from the results of a decade of proprietary research underpinning my book about the issues that knock brands off their feet, *When Growth Stalls* (2009). All of them are practical, and all are put to the test on a regular basis at my own integrated marketing firm, McKee Wallwork & Company, as we revitalize stalled, stuck, and stale brands.

Every one of the most successful brands in the world was, at some point, worth nothing. *Power Branding* helps explain what is it that enables some brands to continually grow bigger and better while others stumble along year after year, running but never winning the race. The difference is that the best brands aren't slaves to conventional marketing wisdom. That gives them a competitive edge that, until now, has been difficult to come by.

In the pages that follow you'll see many of the best practices of the best brands in the world. Some should go without saying, but since they often go without doing, we can all use the reminder. Some will seem counterintuitive. Some you may not agree with or even believe. That's OK. Not all of the principles presented here are applicable to all brands. But if more brands adopted *Power Branding* thinking, not only would their results improve, what we as consumers experience online, on television, and everywhere else we face the endless onslaught of commercial messages would be much more pleasant.

A word about how *Power Branding* is organized. You've heard of the Journalist's Six: who, what, when, where, why and how. They're the elements of information needed to get the full story, whether it's a reporter uncovering a scandal, a detective investigating a crime, or a customer service representative trying to resolve a complaint. There's even an old PR formula that uses them as a template for how to write a news release.

Most of the time it doesn't matter in what order the information is gathered, as long as all six questions are ultimately addressed. The customer service rep's story may begin with who was offended, while the journalist may follow a lead based on what happened. The detective may start with where a crime was committed while details of who and what (not to mention when and why) are still sketchy.

Many marketers instinctively begin with questions about what and where, as in "what" their branding efforts should communicate or "where" they should appear. That's what gets them into trouble. They may have some success putting their plans together by relying on intuition and experience, but both can be misleading in a rapidly changing marketing world. These days it's easy for anyone to become confused by (or fall prey to) the latest and greatest tactics.

The common way of citing the Journalist's Six—who, what, when, where, why, and how—rolls off the tongue and is a great mnemonic device. But unlike in other professions, the development of an effective branding program requires that the six questions be answered in a specific order:

Why → Who → What → How → Where → When

By following this pathway, you can avoid a great deal of confusion, trial and error, and blind alleys, preserving your brand's precious time and resources. Like putting on your socks before your shoes, doing things in order makes all the difference.

The best brands begin by asking "why": Why do we exist? Why is our brand important? Why is investing our limited resources in branding more beneficial than investing in other aspects of our business? These questions, properly considered, force company leaders to clearly define their branding objectives and confront their (often-unrealized) assumptions before they get too far down the road.

The chapters that follow have been organized according to this approach, each offering a power branding principle brought to life by the example of one or more of the world's leading brands. Absorb them all and you'll get a mini-MBA—Master of Brand Administration—that will enable you to achieve your "why" by confidently taking on the other questions:

Who (Audience)—Who is essential to our achieving our goals? To whom should we be directing our message? Whose hearts and minds must we win in order to succeed? The better any company defines its "who"—and the more it can know about their lifestyles, behaviors, attitudes, opinions, wants, and needs—the more effectively its branding efforts can address the remaining Ws.

What (Strategy)—As in "what" your brand must represent to your target audience in order to accomplish your business objectives. This, of course, encompasses a host of decisions, from product to pricing, policy to packaging, and everything in between. But it is also where key branding issues are addressed, including positioning, differentiation, and a determination of the personality dimensions that are appropriate for both the brand and the customer need.

How (Creativity)—Armed with the knowledge of what you want to communicate to whom, next comes the most mysterious aspect of branding: "how." This is where intuition and instinct play as important a role as logic and reason, and where you can easily go wrong if you expect your target audience to be rational, to pay attention, or to give you the credit you deserve. Seldom will they let you in the front door of their minds, so the trick lies in figuring out how to climb through a window.

Where and When (Execution)—The last two questions must be addressed together as you dive into the specifics of execution. The task now revolves around determining the best methods, places, and times to communicate your "what" to your "who" in service of your "why." At this stage you'll be required to make many tactical decisions, but if you've effectively addressed the first four questions, you'll have the context and perspective you need to make the final two work as hard as possible on your behalf.

There's one more important section of the book, which I've affectionately titled "Whoops." Yes, even the best brands step in it occasionally. By learning from their examples, you can save yourself some headaches.

These days it's fashionable to focus on what's current, what's cool, what's next. But there are fundamental, timeless principles of branding that we would all do well to learn. *Power Branding* is not a set of rules to be followed or regulations to be adhered to. It's simply a suite of commonsense, sometimes-counterintuitive principles based on how real humans interact in the real world. As you apply them to your unique set of circumstances, your brand will become more powerful than ever.

WHO

NO BRAND CAN BE ALL THINGS TO ALL PEOPLE. A BRAND, LIKE A beam of light, gains intensity with focus. If you want your brand to be beloved, you must first determine by whom.

1
WHO COMES FIRST

IF YOU WERE A TRENDSETTING, OUTGOING, RISK-TAKING, SPORTS freak of a young man, what would be a great way to spend time with your friends? Buffalo Wild Wings has a suggestion: wings, beer, and the big game at a restaurant designed to provide the ultimate sports experience.

Unlike a lot of other casual dining restaurants, Buffalo Wild Wings clearly knows whom it serves. The chain avoids broad-based discounting, preferring instead to focus on the quality of its food and overall customer experience.[1] It can do so because it knows who its core audience is and doesn't try to attract everyone. That's step one of power branding; the way to have sharp, clean edges in the marketplace is to know whose bell you're trying to ring.

That doesn't mean you can't serve a wide variety of customers; it's not that older men, or women, or nerdy types who otherwise don't fit Buffalo Wild Wings' core target profile don't eat there. But the experience is designed for a unique type of person marked by a well-defined profile that goes well beyond demographics.

Brands often think of their target audience in terms of age, income, and geography, or perhaps education or ethnicity. But people aren't driven by their demographics—not every young man is going to relish hot wings and cold beer at a sports bar, just as not every older woman would avoid them. Demographics tend to correlate with behavior, but they rarely cause it. If someone who doesn't fit the profile of who your brand targets wishes to do business with you, of course you'll take their money. But effective branding is not about whose business you'll accept;

it's about whose business you seek. Buffalo Wild Wings simply won't be as pleasant an experience to those who are introverts, or don't like sports, or are vegetarians—regardless of their age and sex.

A few years back the Zogby organization posed a simple question to consumers: If you could only shop at one department store for the rest of your life, which store would you choose?[2] It's perhaps not surprising that Walmart (26 percent) and Target (22 percent) topped the list, given their ubiquity and affordability—they simply appeal to the broadest cross-section of consumers. And it's also not surprising that Walmart loyalists tend to have lower incomes and are less educated than Target customers—important demographic criteria.

But if you look a little deeper into the data, interesting patterns emerge. For example, Walmart shoppers reported that they traveled less and tended to favor a Republican presidential candidate. Target shoppers said they traveled more and leaned toward a Democratic candidate. Those two characteristics say as much about who those stores' customers are as their income and education profile does.

> If you try to be all things to all people, you'll end up being nothing to anybody.

Now throw other retailers into the mix. Costco loyalists look more like Target shoppers in terms of income, travel profile, and political views, whereas Sears' shoppers are older, more conservative, and even more likely than Walmart customers to own a home and a gun.

My point isn't to suggest that these retailers should build their appeal around singular dimensions such as political leanings, travel habits, or gun ownership (the Zogby poll didn't go into the specific depth that a custom brand identity exploration would). But the study does support the idea that people's varying behaviors, lifestyles, and leanings lead them to naturally gravitate to one brand over another—even in somewhat commoditized categories. There's not a brand on the planet that can't leverage that powerful truth.

If you seek to be a great brand, first determine who you want to think of you as one. And be careful that you don't take the easy road and make assumptions based on demographics alone. Sure, better-educated people are likely to be more knowledgeable consumers in general, but don't think for a minute that, say, a fourth-generation farmer who has only an eighth-grade education can't make a more sophisticated purchase decision about a new tractor than a PhD professor of agriculture. There's much more to people than meets the demographer's eye.

2

SMALL MEANS BIG

AS BUFFALO WILD WINGS' EXAMPLE SHOWS, THE MORE YOU want to enhance the power of your brand, the better you must understand just who it is you're trying to reach. And here's an important corollary: The narrower your target, the greater the intensity of your brand's appeal can be.

Mountain Dew, originally named after a slang term for moonshine, was first positioned as a hillbilly soft drink. For years it languished as such and as an also-ran in a category filled with big-spending competitors. But in 1993, the "Do the Dew" campaign appeared with a focus on what the company calls "Dew Dudes"—young, active, X Games–type men. Since that time, Mountain Dew has taken off to become the number four soft drink in terms of market share—behind Coke, Pepsi, and Diet Coke and ahead of Diet Pepsi, Sprite, and Dr Pepper.[1]

How to explain Mountain Dew's success? It narrowed its target so it could increase the intensity of appeal. By focusing only on active, thrill-seeking young men, Mountain Dew could create compelling messaging just for them.

By sponsoring snowboarders and skateboarders rather than basketball stars and baseball players, Mountain Dew has clearly staked its turf, sponsoring the first-ever X Games back in 1995 and producing its own snowboarding movie, *First Descent*. The brand sponsors a professional skate team and has a YouTube channel called "How We DEW" that features the exploits of its athletes.

Further building on its branding success, Mountain Dew even curates a record label, Green Label Sound, with the goal of raising the profile of independent artists. It sponsors Green-Label.com, a branded content site designed to be a hub for youth culture. And in partnership with Burton, a popular snowboarding brand, it launched the Green Mountain Project, recycling plastic soda bottles and spinning the pellets into yarn that's woven through the fabric of an outerwear collection supported by the tagline "Drink it. Recycle it. Wear it." Now, that's brand loyalty.

What Mountain Dew has achieved as a brand would have been impossible if it tried to win market share by appealing to the broadest possible audience.

Credit card companies have understood this principle for years, targeting increasingly narrow audiences in an effort to boost their brands' relevance. They offer cards targeted specifically to university alumni, fans of Disneyland, Sam's Club shoppers, and members of AARP. They even offer cards for home mortgages and health savings accounts. If there's an affinity group or a usage occasion, it's a fair bet that a credit card is targeted to it.

> **The narrower your target, the greater the intensity of your brand's appeal.**

When auto industry icon Bob Lutz was at Chrysler, he believed that it would be better to design cars that were at the top of the wish list of a quarter of the population than models that were somewhere down the list for everyone. On his watch, Chrysler developed the PT Cruiser, the Jeep Grand Cherokee, the popular Dodge Ram pickup, and the head-turning Dodge Viper. His strategy reinvigorated Chrysler and helped turn the company's fortunes around.

And then there's Ferrari, the ultimate ride for many sports car enthusiasts. After a particularly good sales year, the company made the strategic decision to reduce the number of cars it would allow dealers to sell. Ferrari chairman Luca di Montezemolo said of the decision, "Those who buy a Ferrari buy a dream, and they must be reassured that their dream of exclusivity will be fulfilled."[2]

If it's true for soft drinks, credit cards, and automobiles, it can be true for your brand as well. If you narrow your focus to a key audience defined not merely by demographics but by lifestyle, attitudes, perceptions, behaviors, or anything else relevant to the purchase occasion, you may just make your brand an integral part of their lives.

3

HAPPY ARE THE HUNTED

SO HOW, EXACTLY, DOES A BRAND DEVELOP THE DEEP UNDER-standing of its target audience that lets it build equity like Buffalo Wild Wings or Mountain Dew? By first looking inward.

Tony Hsieh, founder and chief inspiration officer at Zappos, famously made the observation that Zappos isn't a shoe company, it's a customer service company that happens to sell shoes. And from the day he launched Zappos, Hsieh put his money where his mouth was, making ordering easy, returns hassle-free, and shunning industry conventions like tracking how quickly customer service representatives handle telephone inquiries. At Zappos, people who pick up the phone understand they're to spend all the time they need to delight those who place the calls.

Still, despite a great track record and growing reputation, from the get-go Zappos faced extreme competition from retailers (both online and off) that weren't going to cede their fans without a fight. The company was growing, but it knew it needed to do a better job communicating to shoe shoppers what its brand was about. But almost everyone buys shoes; how was Zappos to determine where to find its most likely prospective customers? How could the company find its version of "Dew Dudes"?

> Somebody loves you. The trick is to figure out who
> they are so you can find more of them.

By studying some 900,000 of its most loyal customers, Zappos was able to develop a profile of what it came to call "Happy Hunters" who shared similar age, income, behavioral, and (most importantly) attitudinal characteristics.[1] To Happy Hunters, time is more valuable than money, shopping online makes them feel more productive, and they place a premium on customer service. Zappos calculated that there were more than 7 million Happy Hunters as yet untapped by the brand. Now that's a target audience.

The company and its ad agency used that insight in the development of a multimedia campaign that further raised awareness of the brand, generated powerful results on key branding metrics, and kept the revenue curve sloping upward. Not coincidentally, Tony Hsieh shortly thereafter released his bestselling book, *Delivering Happiness*.

You may not have a million customer records to parse, but you can benefit from the same principle. No matter how big or small your brand, if you've been in business for any length of time, you must be doing something right. Somehow, some way, some customers found their way to your door and liked what you had to offer.

The best thing you can do to grow is to find out who they are and why your brand rings their bell. Then go about finding more of them. And unless your media budget is big enough that you've already reached everyone in the world, there are always more.

I once sat incredulous in a client's conference room when a research company told the brand managers that since they were doing well with x-type customers, they should now go after y-type customers. It was a crazy recommendation. Not only might x and y customer types be like oil and water (in this case, they were), it would be less efficient for the company to spend its resources and potentially dilute its brand pursuing two different targets (unless they're not really different after all, a topic we'll take up in the next chapter).

Every brand has its own Happy Hunters, however it defines them. If you haven't yet figured out who you want to pursue, take a look at who has pursued you. Sometimes love is right under your nose.

4

UNCOMMON IS COMMON

FINE, YOU SAY. MOUNTAIN DEW WAS ABLE TO IDENTIFY A NAR-
row target audience that would mainline caffeine if it could. And Zappos
identified a single target profile with an untapped market of 7 million
people. But my business isn't so simple. My brand has multiple target
audiences to which it has to appeal.

No, it doesn't. In fact, it can't. Let me clarify with an example.

Almost 30 years ago, in his first radio recording session for Motel 6,
humorist Tom Bodett ad-libbed a line that has gone down in advertising
history: "We'll leave the light on for you." Those seven words encourage
listeners to envision ways in which the folks at Motel 6 will welcome
weary travelers, making sure the sheets are clean, rooms are safe, and
whatever else they care to imagine.

The campaign has been wildly successful, earning more than 150
awards over its long run. It didn't hurt Tom Bodett's career either, who
was building houses in 1986 when the Motel 6 call came—he was chosen, he says, because he sounded like the person who stays there.[1]

Sounds simple, right? Just like Mountain Dew and Zappos, Motel 6
seems to have found a single, narrow target around which it built a great
branding campaign. Not so fast.

The Richards Group, the Dallas-based advertising agency that
originally developed the idea, faced a tough challenge when it got the
Motel 6 assignment, as the chain's guests fell into three very different categories: seniors, vacationing families, and self-paying business
travelers. How to make one motel chain appeal to old people on fixed
incomes, harried parents with demanding kids, and haggard business

travelers who just need a place to crash for the night—now that was a challenge.

But the agency didn't throw up its hands. Instead, applying the same principle Zappos would years later, it determined to look deeper into the psyches of the variety of Motel 6 customers and see if it could find something they had in common. Sure enough, despite their visible differences, Motel 6 customers all had a self-image of being frugal, which, according to an agency spokesperson, "represents the common denominator that predicts their behavior regardless of age, income, traveling purpose or any of a hundred other things that make each guest different."[2]

> No matter how different your customers appear,
> they have your brand in common. Find out why.

Based on that realization, down-home radio personality Tom Bodett, who was able to relate to all types of Motel 6 guests, got his big break. Here's how, two decades later, he describes (with his now-legendary laconic humor) the brand's cross-target appeal:

> Americans are generally very self-sufficient and I think generally averse to pretension just as I am. When you point out that you don't need to have art on your motel room walls because your eyes are closed anyway, or that you can take the money you save from not having avocado body balm in the bathroom swag basket and go buy some real chips and dip—avocado body balm, by the way, tastes just like soap—people respond. People feel vulnerable when they travel. Nobody wants to be taken advantage of or talked into something they don't want. Staying at Motel 6 makes you feel smarter.[3]

That's a truth that can ring the bell of a variety of seemingly different audiences—be they senior citizens, families with children, or self-paying business travelers. None of them wants to feel vulnerable. All of them want to feel smart. That's how Motel 6 found its target.

That's not to say that no company has legitimately different target audiences that have little in common or even conflicting or contradictory needs. In that case, a single brand won't work. That's why Procter & Gamble makes several different brands of laundry detergent: Tide for superior cleaning, Dreft for sensitive baby skin, Gain for fragrance, Era for stain fighting, Cheer for color protection—you get the idea. Multiple needs, multiple targets, multiple brands. It's an effective—though expensive—approach to branding.

Fortunately, most companies don't have to go down the multi-brand road. More often than not, what your various target audiences have in common outweighs their differences; after all, at some level your value equation already adds up for each of them or you wouldn't consider them your target audiences.

I rarely stay in a Motel 6 because, based on my wants and needs, I'm not really who they're after. Nor do I fit the Mountain Dew profile in terms of my age or lifestyle. But that doesn't mean you'll never find me chugging a Dew or hoping the manager at Motel 6 leaves the light on for me. By focusing narrowly and increasing the intensity of their appeal, brands sometimes win the business of even people who don't fit the mold.

5

IT'S NOT ABOUT YOU

WE'VE ESTABLISHED THAT IDENTIFYING A NARROW, WELL-defined target audience is step one. But here's a tough question: Even if you've done so, why would you expect members of that audience to give your brand the time of day?

I recently heard a radio commercial advertising an automotive summer maintenance check. The ad talked about all of the things a particular service center could do to get my car ready for the season. But as far as I knew, my car needed none of those things. Like most people, I tend to not think about maintenance for my car until it's broken. Car problems aren't car problems until they become car problems. This ad was offering to solve a problem I didn't know I had.

When an ad is about your brand, you're essentially asking people to actively pay attention, process what you're telling them, and compare it to their current reality to see if it fits. On occasion you may hit someone who's in the purchase-decision mode and tell them exactly what they need to hear, but most of the time your ad will fall on deaf ears.

By contrast, if you begin with your target audience and understand what's on their minds and where they're coming from, you're much more likely to capture their attention. You'll get credit for understanding them, and they'll give you a chance to make a point that they can grasp. The key is to start from their perspective, not yours.

The standard-bearer for this type of approach is Nike. Most people can't honestly say that Nike really makes a better shoe than its competitors. Is its cushioning more resilient? Its arch support stronger? Its durability longer lasting?

I have no idea, and I'll bet you don't either. Yet Nike holds a commanding lead in its industry because decades ago it perfected a customer-centric kind of advertising—one that focused not on a product but on an idea. Nike signed Michael Jordan in 1984, introduced its "Just Do It" campaign in 1988, and has been chased by its competitors ever since.

Nike's approach has become a benchmark in the world of branding and its tagline a mantra in the culture at large. The reason is simple: "Just Do It" is a concept virtually anyone can relate to, from the couch potato for whom "just do it" means taking a walk, to the elite athlete for whom it means competing in an ultramarathon.

It's not the slogan itself that's important; it's the universal idea that the slogan so plainly articulates. Nike's three-word turn-of-phrase represents a spirit that inspires the athlete within us all, calling us to take just a single next (or first) step. There is almost nobody who can't do that. (Which, by the way, wins Nike the prize for identifying its "who" as well—the brand found an incredibly broad target audience that feels incredibly narrow.)

> **If you want someone to take an interest in**
> **your brand, take an interest in them first.**

In one notable Nike commercial, Spike Lee watches with incredulity a high-flying Michael Jordan and blurts out, "It must be the shoes!" But as the director as well as the co-star of the commercial, Lee knew it wasn't about the shoes at all. It was about the idea that Nike was selling—an idea that people were buying, again and again. The secret to Nike's success in branding has always been to make the message about its customer, not about Nike.

How might the automotive repair shop have applied this lesson? Well, any number of ideas related to cars and summer driving are common to us all, from sweltering seats, to inefficient air conditioners, to annoying tailgaters. The first thing this brand should do is tap into the universal experience of driving a car. It should spend its efforts relating to its target audience in a way that makes them want to listen—with an insightful observation, perhaps, or a common driving complaint, or maybe even a witty or snarky remark about traffic hassles. By drawing them in and finding a point of connection, prospective customers will be more likely to pay attention and think of the brand as a company they can relate to. When the inevitable car problem does arise, a brand like that will be more likely to get their business.

It's an odd, counterintuitive principle of good branding that the best way to sell something is to quit selling. Start relating instead. As you do, you'll find that people are more apt to listen, more certain to develop affection for your brand, and more likely to buy what you have to offer.

6

HEART BEATS WALLET

NEW CUSTOMERS ARE VITAL, BUT BRAND LOYALTY IS THE KEY TO profitability. It costs a lot more money to attract a customer than to keep one, and it's those repeat transactions that fill the bottom line with beautiful black ink.

As a result, many brands implement so-called relationship marketing programs that measure loyalty primarily by transactions. But that's where the law of unintended consequences steps in, as such programs tend to attract those customers whose affection can be bought, actually hindering the brand's ability to identify, understand, and nurture its most truly loyal customers.

If a company focuses on share of wallet, it may or may not gain share of heart, but the reverse is almost always true. One Australian study found that while 80 percent of consumers buy more from retailers with loyalty programs, fewer than half feel more loyal to those brands.[1]

How does a company ensure that its loyalty program achieves effective share of heart? Here are a few principles to consider.

The first may sound odd to those who work so hard trying to create committed customers: Loyalty is natural. Think about it. We're loyal to sports teams, actors, and political parties. We're loyal to cars, shoes, pubs, and pizza joints. When we identify with someone or something, we want desperately to reinforce the credibility of our beliefs, and one way we do that is by forming loyalties to them. So we give those brands repeat business and brag about them to our friends.

If a brand serves its customers well and meets their expectations the old-fashioned way, then some amount of natural loyalty will result. And attempts to "buy" more—the functional equivalent of paying someone to go on a second date—might actually backfire. We need to look for ways to stimulate the growth of natural loyalty rather than taking short-cuts that focus only on behavior.

Why do people become loyal fans of actors and musicians? What's the rationale behind caring who wins *American Idol* or the World Series? There really isn't one, which leads to the second principle: True loyalty comes from the heart.

We care about performers because we empathize with them. They lay themselves out for us—whether it's an actor demonstrating raw emotion, a musician performing passionately, or an athlete leaving it all on the field. The common thread is vulnerability; the willingness to expose themselves and take a risk. And that creates a heartfelt response that makes us want to attend the movie, download the album, or sit in subzero temperatures watching the game (at full price, mind you). Our behavior arises not out of rationality but personality. The Coca-Colas, Targets, and Starbucks of the world understand this and have built their brands accordingly.

Loyalty is a state of mind, not a share of wallet.

Which brings me to a third point: Loyalty takes time to develop. My firm recently hit the annual renewal cycle for our company credit cards, and we decided we should shop around to see if we could avoid paying a fee. It didn't take us long to find a handful of good options offered by Visa, MasterCard, and American Express.

At first I didn't have a preference, as all three cards included loyalty program benefits. But then I got to thinking about how we use our cards. When we buy office equipment or books online, it doesn't matter what type of card we use. But when I take a client or prospect out to dinner and reach for my wallet, there's a certain statement that I want to make. Once I thought about the decision that way, my choice was easy: American Express.

I'm not saying the other brands don't have value or that rewards programs can't be difference makers. What I am saying is that a physical reward can be matched a lot more easily than can the cachet American Express built up over decades with its comparatively high annual fee, exclusive Gold (then Platinum and Black) cards, and long-running "Don't leave home without it" campaign.

Finally, just because you can't precisely measure something (or measure it easily) doesn't mean it's not working. Behavior tends to get measured because it can be measured. But measurement can create its own reality and cause the loyalty marketing focus to become too narrowly defined. It's not that behavior isn't important (repeat transactions are ultimately the point), but efforts focused on the "why" of behavior rather than the "what" are more likely to be successful in the long term. Attitudes and beliefs can be difficult to grasp and even harder to track, but they lie at the root of true loyalty.

Technology has changed a great deal over the past several years, enabling a whole new world of customer intimacy and communication. But human nature doesn't change—people still want to be valued as individuals, and they want to protect their privacy. Just because a company can do something doesn't mean it should.

The best brands do their best to ensure that every contact with their company offers a psychic reward, not just a physical one. Find out what your customers really value. Never violate their trust or sense of security. Make it your objective to build not only short-term transactions but long-term affection as well. That affection will pay off long after the points and perks expire.

7

RELATIONSHIPS ARE
RECIPROCAL

THE IDEA THAT A BRAND COULD GENERATE LONG-TERM AFFEC-
tion is as intimidating as it is powerful. How on earth to go about it?
Well, the principles of power branding aren't mysteries; in fact, they reflect the principles of any healthy relationship. To paraphrase the title
of a famous book, just about all you need to know about branding you
learned in kindergarten.

Think back to when you were a kid confiding in your best friend.
"I'll tell you a secret if you tell me one." You wouldn't reveal yourself or
give out the dirt without collecting some dirt on your buddy. That was
the only way to ensure he didn't use the information to humiliate you. It
was the doctrine of Mutually Assured Destruction writ small.

That's the way relationships grow—through give-and-take. Relationships develop only so far as trust develops. And trust develops only
by mutual disclosure and the circumspect protection of valuable information. Relationships are reciprocal, and they require investment.

Years ago I was a long-haired, bearded 22-year-old with a lousy
job that paid irregularly. I was also engaged to be married and preoccupied with becoming responsible, not to mention passing muster with
my soon-to-be father-in-law. That meant, among other things, securing
life insurance to take care of my bride if some tragedy were to befall her
prince.

It was about then that a Northwestern Mutual Life insurance agent
named David Bernard was referred to me. David was older than me, and

I remember being mystified as to why he would waste his time patiently explaining to a young kid with few prospects the difference between whole life and term insurance. I didn't know anything about the insurance business, even less about Northwestern Mutual. Based on the puny premiums I'd be paying, I knew neither the company nor David was going to get rich on me.

Fast-forward several years. David is still my insurance agent. Northwestern Mutual is still my insurance company. The insurance portfolio David helped me build over the years has become somewhat sizable. Over the past two decades or so, he and I have played basketball together, our wives have volunteered together, and our daughters took dance class together. David and I once found ourselves whiling away the hours sharing driving duties in a 26-foot semi filled with props for a ballet performance.

> **Trust is built on familiarity. And destroyed by exploitation.**

Although my relationship with David is unique, our story is not. I invested with him because he invested in me. Our relationship was, from the start, reciprocal.

For all human history, business has been based on this principle. Buyers and sellers have followed a similar pattern of nurturing family and community ties as they traded. Commerce has always been based on proximity and goodwill. Mistrust has always been destructive.

Today, the web has made the world a smaller place, and social media has enhanced the ability of buyers and sellers to form relationships. Proximity is global for many products and services. But building goodwill remains (perhaps more than ever) a challenge. While a variety of digital marketing tools can facilitate customer relationship development, they can also foster mistrust if used hastily or improperly.

Today we know so much about our customers that it's tempting not only to congratulate them on their most recent purchase but also to send them a birthday card, offer condolences about a death in the family, and wish them well in their pregnancy or good luck in their new job. But relationships are reciprocal; if a brand oversteps the (explicit or implied) bounds of permission it has to use customer data, it can easily lose trust.

The more time you invest in getting to know your target audience, the deeper and richer—and, most likely, bigger—your customer base will grow. It has never been so easy for businesses to reach out to prospective customers, and never have there been so many tools by which we can accelerate relationship development. But if your brand is perceived as being invasive, manipulative, or deceptive in any way—not just what it says, but where, when, and how it says it—you can quickly see its equity evaporate.

8

IRRATIONAL IS RATIONAL

AUTOMOBILES ARE REMARKABLE THINGS. THOUSANDS OF pounds of sheet metal, rubber, plastic, copper, iron, and who-knows-what-else are carefully shaped, molded, and fitted together to create machines that safely and comfortably hurl our frail bodies from one place to another at speeds unimaginable by our great-great-grandparents. Different models can be evaluated and compared according to literally hundreds of detailed specifications.

Automobiles are also very expensive, which increases the risk of buying the wrong one. If ever there was a purchase occasion that should be driven by rationality, buying an automobile is it. But we all know that's not the case. As the automakers know, it's as much—if not more—about image.

It wasn't so long ago that Toyota chairman Eiji Toyoda determined it was time for his company to build a world-class luxury car. Wisely understanding that the Toyota brand would, especially at that time, not naturally be equated with luxury, the first LS 400 was launched in 1989 under an all-new badge: Lexus. Brand Lexus has enjoyed consistent success since its launch, in part because of deft messaging that has continually reinforced the idea behind its original tagline, "The relentless pursuit of perfection."

Why, exactly, do people buy the Lexus brand? No doubt loyalists can cite dozens of rational reasons why the cars meet their standards. But most luxury cars meet most of the same standards. Those brands that, like Lexus, enjoy the most success understand that very few decisions car buyers make are fully rational.

That's OK. Choices that aren't based exclusively on reason and logic are extremely common, no less legitimate, and in many cases better than decisions arrived at through extensive reasoning. In fact, research from Cornell University psychologists demonstrates that subconscious feelings often lead to better decision making when people choose apartments, vacation destinations, and, yes, cars.[1]

It's not easy to say why, because the nonrational part of the brain works in mysterious ways. In a 2007 Harvard study, for example, hotel room attendants who were told they were getting a good workout and burning lots of calories at their jobs actually lowered their body fat and blood pressure at greater rates than those who weren't told that, a finding that reveals how expectations can play a role in physiology.[2]

Similarly, in 2011, University of Michigan psychologists found that students' enjoyment of the last of five different-flavor Hershey's Kisses was much greater when they were told the one they were eating was "the last one" rather than "the next one."[3] And a 2009 Caltech study demonstrated that people believe expensive wines taste better, even when the prices of Cabernets ranging from $5 to $90 were randomly mixed.[4] These studies reveal an interesting link between expectations and perceived value—a link brands like Lexus have used to great advantage.

> **People don't always know why they do what they do.**
> **But that doesn't make them irrational.**

All of which brings up a few interesting questions. Is the value of something in the thing itself or in the benefits (real and perceived) it provides? Why is a "perceived" benefit any less valuable than a "real" benefit? And how do consumers' rational calculations interact with their nonrational instincts to lead them to the choices they make? We don't fully know, but Professor Gerd Gigerenzer of the Max Planck Institute for Human Development sums up the state of our current understanding when he says, "Neither extreme of hyper-rationality or irrationality captures the essence of human reasoning."[5]

Indeed. We all use intuitive and subconscious—nonrational—shortcuts every day. We call them instinct or hunches or gut feelings because we don't know what else to label them. But simply because we don't understand how they work doesn't mean they aren't legitimate and valuable functions of our miraculous minds.

Professor Gigerenzer even submits that excess information can make a decision worse by hindering our ability to focus on its most critical aspects, citing sports as an example.

"Consider how players catch a ball," Gigerenzer says. "It may seem that they would have to solve complex differential equations in their heads to predict the trajectory of the ball. In fact, players use a simple heuristic. When a ball comes in high, the player fixates the ball and starts running. The heuristic is to adjust the running speed so that the angle of gaze remains constant—that is, the angle between the eye and the ball. The player can ignore all the information necessary to compute the trajectory, such as the ball's initial velocity, distance, and angle, and just focus on one piece of information, the angle of gaze."[6]

That's a mouthful, and while I don't understand the physics of a fly ball, I don't have to—precisely Gigerenzer's point. As marketers, we don't have to plumb the mysterious depths of the mind as we go about pitching our brands. But we should neither presume consumers are making fully rational calculations based on articulated benefits nor dismiss their abilities to take intuitive shortcuts based on experience, emotions, and aesthetics.

We have a long way to go before we fully understand how the mind works. In the meantime, suffice it to say the marketplace is neither a courtroom nor a crapshoot. It's more like a carnival, through which people are as likely to find their way by the sights, sounds, and smells they encounter as they are by a map. If in your branding efforts you recognize that imagery is as important as information, you'll ensure people can both appreciate the experience and enjoy the ride.

9

CUSTOMERS AREN'T ALWAYS RIGHT

ALL RELATIONSHIPS REQUIRE SOME AMOUNT OF GIVE-AND-TAKE. Never is one party always right and another always wrong. As the saying goes, it takes two to tango (and, in the case of a disagreement, two to tangle).

That's why the old saying "The customer is always right" is so misleading. It's not that we shouldn't listen to customers or place special emphasis on understanding their wants and needs, concerns and complaints. It's that we must do so with discernment. Not only are your customers not always rational, they're not always right. And sometimes they're just plain wrong.

When the Apple Macintosh was first released, Steve Jobs said, "We built [the Mac] for ourselves. We were the group of people who were going to judge whether it was great or not. We weren't going to do market research."[1] Years later he echoed his remarks: "A lot of times, people don't know what they want until you show it to them."[2] Very few companies have the creativity, insight, and tenacity that Apple under Jobs did, but his points are well taken: If Apple had depended on customers to tell it what to do, I daresay there would be no Apple today.

That thinking applies to customer service as much as it does to research and development (R&D). We've all heard or experienced horror stories of disgruntled customers whose anger turns to abuse. It's a good idea to be willing to walk as far as possible down the mea culpa road with these customers, as long as you draw the line, politely but firmly, when their behavior offends other customers or threatens your staff. The very nature of such interactions makes them easy to recognize.

Here are a few additional, subtler instances in which you might want to think twice about how much you listen to the voice of the customer.

When they can't know. Your customers know less about the science behind your offering than you do. That means their perceptions of what they want are firmly grounded in what they think is possible rather than what is truly possible.

> **Asking your customers is one of the surest ways to get it right. Or wrong.**

A century ago, nobody who sat atop a horse-drawn carriage thought to ask for a Model-T. A generation ago, nobody who used a pay phone had any idea how soon they would become obsolete. I certainly think teleportation would beat wedging my way into a crowded airplane seat; as far as I know, that's still in the realm of science fiction, and I wouldn't even think to suggest it to an airline during a telephone survey.

When they won't say. Sometimes customers believe they can gain the upper hand in a transaction by being coy. For instance, a good salesperson can walk a prospect through a series of questions designed to lead them to purchase; handled with subtlety, this is an effective way to move someone along. Handled clumsily, however, it raises suspicions and can cause prospects to provide misinformation, from the wrong zip code to a phony phone number.

Seeking the voice of the customer in branding can be even more misleading. As my colleague Daniel Andreani quipped: "Asking a consumer about his opinion of your advertising is like asking a deer about the best way to hunt it."

Customers can unintentionally lead us astray as well, such as when we ask them to predict their future behavior. Research subjects have been wrong on many things, from New Coke (they gave it a thumbs up) to the Sony Walkman (they gave it a thumbs down). These days, study after study shows that people are willing to pay more for environmentally friendly product options. Real-world analysis of their behavior demonstrates that few put their money where their mouths are.

When they won't let up. As Adam Smith pointed out: "It is not from the benevolence of the butcher, the brewer or the baker that we expect our dinner, but from their regard to their own self interest."[3] The same is true of the people who purchase the meat, the beer, and the bread. If you ask customers to design the perfect product, they'll rack up the features and ratchet down the price, then be thrilled to buy from you all the way through your "Going out of Business" sale.

It's a safe bet that if you're not losing some customers because your prices are too high, your prices are too low. I know how hard it is to watch customers walk out the door because they don't like how much you charge, but the price can be right for them only if it's right for you too. Someone has to look out for the best interests of the business. No matter how much your customers love you, it ain't gonna be them.

Always take the voice of the customer with a grain of salt. Customers can offer valuable and insightful information, to be sure, but ultimately they work for themselves, not you. There's nothing cynical or antagonistic about that; it's simply the way the marketplace works. The more you know about customers' interests, the better you'll be able to act in your own.

10
RESEARCH CAN BE DECEIVING

IN 1986 STEVE JOBS PURCHASED THE COMPUTER GRAPHICS DIVI-
sion from Lucasfilm and christened it Pixar. Less than a decade
of experimentation later, Pixar released *Toy Story*, the world's first
computer-animated feature film. It was the highest-grossing film of
the year and won accolades and awards from across the spectrum of
moviegoers.

That same year Pixar went public and went on to produce a host of
hits, from *Monsters, Inc.*, to *Finding Nemo, The Incredibles, Cars, WALL-
E*, and *Up*. Pixar has built such a powerful brand that having its impri-
matur on a film virtually guarantees big box office.

Andrew Stanton, director of *Finding Nemo* and *WALL-E*, once a
bit sheepishly admitted, "We selfishly make movies for ourselves that
happen to be juvenile enough that they cover the kids' interests. We've
learned to trust our own instincts about what we like and not rely on, or
trust, what the outside world tells us is going to work."[1]

The artists at Pixar, like the artists at Apple, aren't slaves to market
research. Neither should any brand be. Research can't predict the kind of
cars we will be interested in years from now, how an ad concept will be
received months from now, or what the next hit movie or popular fashion trend will be. Yet we still hold onto hope that somehow statistics and
spreadsheets will enable us to foresee the future. They won't. They can't.

Adrian Van Hooydonk, director of design at BMW, once explained
how the carmaker evaluates vehicle prototypes: "We don't use customer
clinics. They will be judging it based on the world today. Design needs

to look good in eight years' time. You can't ask a customer whether he will like the design of the car in 2018."[2]

Similarly, Lenny Marsh, the father of Snapple, relished his job as the chief new product taster at the company. "If we like it, they'll like it," he would say. "We don't need a focus group. We are a focus group." He must have been doing something right; Snapple became such a hit for its wacky flavors that 22 years after he founded the company, Marsh sold it for a cool $1.7 billion.[3]

Ford famously passed on launching the minivan. Hal Sperlich, who ended up taking the concept to Chrysler, recounted to *Fortune* that Ford balked because research couldn't prove there was a market for such an unprecedented vehicle: "In 10 years of developing the minivan we never once got a letter from a housewife asking us to invent one."[4]

Google once asked users how many results they'd like to see on one screen. People naturally said "more." When Google tripled the number of results, however, it found that traffic actually declined. Not only did the results take a fraction of a second longer to load, but having more options led people to click on links that were less relevant. The respondents in Google's research didn't intentionally lead researchers down the wrong path; they just didn't understand the real-world implications of their choices.

> **Research is a compass, not a map.**

For any research to be scientifically reliable, every variable other than the one being tested must be controlled. But in most marketing research, it's impossible to control all of the variables, which means a certain amount of error is embedded in the results of every study. Where that error lies, and how significantly it affects the outcome, is always a mystery. That's what makes it so dangerous.

Even if all of the variables could be controlled, it doesn't change the fact that people don't—or can't—always tell the truth.

"I will never have a cell phone." That's a direct quote from my wife, who also said she'd never use the Internet. Today she sent me a text message complaining that Facebook is acting funny again. She didn't mean to lie. She's just not an early adopter. And she can't predict how she will respond to new developments in the future. None of us can.

Harris Interactive conducted a study about personal consumer behavior, with half the respondents surveyed online and half on the phone. The results demonstrated that online respondents tended to be more honest, whereas phone respondents were more likely to provide what they thought was the "correct" answer. People interviewed via phone were more likely than their online counterparts to say they were weekly churchgoers, give money to charity, exercise regularly, and brush their teeth twice a day. And fewer admitted they gambled. Shocking.

Sometimes people won't accurately describe their wants, needs, or behavior, and sometimes they simply can't. As David Lewis, chief designer at Bang & Olufsen, put it, "You can't go out and ask people what they need or want, because they don't know. The whole trick is to come out with a product and say, 'Have you thought of this?' and hear the consumer respond, 'Wow! No, I hadn't.' If you can do that, you're on."[5]

How much do you love your spouse? What's the "value" of poetry? What is a life worth? Some things just can't be quantified. Yet in business, we often act as if everything can be. Market research is a compass, not a map—it can give you a sense of where your brand is, but it can't tell you where to take it.

11
IT'S NOT THE SHOES

ONE OF THE REASONS WE SHOULD BE WARY OF RESEARCH DONE wrong is our own individual consumer confusion. Sometimes we don't even know how we're going to make a purchase decision until we're in the midst of it.

Years ago, when my son signed up for his first YMCA basketball team, I took him to the mall to buy basketball shoes. I don't know which one of us was more excited. Even though I had a sense (since confirmed) that he wouldn't be headed to the NBA, there's still something special about the wide-eyed dreams of a child.

We got to the store and began scanning the huge array of styles and colors covering the walls. Since he was only seven, I wasn't too concerned about the quality of the insole. He wasn't going to be practicing for hours on end. I also wasn't worried about durability; he would grow out of the shoes before they wore out. And I certainly didn't want to pay too much, figuring my money would be put to better use earning interest in his college fund. But I wanted him to enjoy the moment, so I thought I'd let him pick a pair he liked.

It wasn't long before he pulled some shoes off the wall and looked up at me expectantly. I have to admit, the shoes looked like they'd make him a man among boys on the court. They were black and red mid-rise high-tops, with beefy soles and that famous swoosh on the side. Much to my delight, the price wouldn't require me to take out a second mortgage. But as I reached out to inspect them more closely, I saw two words on the label that took me aback: Dennis. Rodman.

You may not be entirely familiar with the Worm, as they used to call Rodman, but he was one of the NBA's all-time bad boys. Known for wacky haircuts and bad sportsmanship, he knew how to get face time on *SportsCenter*. But he was no role model for kids, and I was not going to allow my son to wear his shoes, even if at his tender age he had no idea who Dennis Rodman was.

I suddenly found myself keenly interested in which shoes my son would pick next. A whole new consideration was added to the purchase decision, and my eyes began to scan the shelves in search of a more appropriate fit. Within seconds, I found a pair of shoes named for another basketball great, Grant Hill. The shoes weren't as attractive as the Rodman version, but Hill was a model NBA citizen, and that was good enough for me. I have no idea whether his shoes were better than Rodman's, they weren't as cool-looking, and they were from a brand I had barely heard of: Fila. But I was operating in an emotional condition that completely reframed my purchase decision.

> **The purchase process itself can change the purchase process.**

This experience may have been extreme in terms of how dominant a role my emotions played, but I don't think it was odd that they factored into the decision. In fact, making purchases based on emotion is quite normal. From the persona of an athlete associated with shoes, to the warm feelings tied to a greeting card brand, to the security of having all-wheel drive (even if you never use it), emotions always play a role in the decisions buyers make.

Crazy, isn't it? But that's how we're made. We're emotional beings, and we respond to emotional appeals. That's why politicians are much more effective telling stories than quoting statistics. The statistics may be incorrect but the stories ring true.

Too many brands fall for what I call the "fallacy of rationality." That's when you believe that if you just present the rational benefits of your product—the better mousetrap—the world will beat a path to your door. Sure, features, benefits, and cost/value equations enter into it, but never do they do all the heavy lifting. I can't think of a single purchase occasion that's completely rational. Show me a purchase made for 100 percent logical reasons, and I'll show you a purchaser who is proud of his rationality—pride being the operative (and emotional) word.

Brands that face a high degree of competitive parity—whose ad budgets depend on what competitors spend—in categories such as basketball shoes, beer, and potato chips understand that the entry to effective differentiation is often achieved through the personality door. They simply don't have unique rational claims to make, so they have to win hearts more than minds. But all brands, and all products—no matter the industry—can leverage the power of personality to strengthen their appeal.

A feature can always be matched. A claim can always be mimicked. But an emotional sweet spot is something your brand can occupy all by itself.

12

SELF-EXPRESSION DOESN'T SELL

GEICO KNOWS ALL ABOUT EMOTIONAL SWEET SPOTS. THE COMpany has always had a pretty simple sales pitch: Save 15 percent or more on car insurance. What the brand has wisely avoided, however, is the assumption that its audience is willing to listen.

Car insurance is, after all, not a particularly appealing subject. Most of us would rather avoid thinking about it most of the time. So instead of getting in our faces with its message, GEICO recognizes that it first must earn the right to be heard. It's not just about making the pitch; it's making the pitch heard. Hence geckos and cavemen and a wry sense of humor that reaches out to its target and offers it something in exchange for listing to the message (relationships are reciprocal, remember?).

Contrast that with what might be called "bumper sticker branding," where marketers just blurt out what they think with little regard for what their prospects will hear. So often—and so easily—their messages can be misunderstood.

A colleague once told me that she went out with a man who had one of those bumper stickers on which an ersatz Calvin (from the comic strip *Calvin and Hobbes*) was relieving himself on a Florida State University logo. When the guy called her for a second date, she declined. It wasn't that she had an affinity for Florida State; it was just that (in her words), "I thought, clearly I can't have anything in common with someone who voluntarily drove himself to the store, purchased that sticker, and applied it to the back of his vehicle."

That's one of the problems with bumper stickers. The man who put Calvin on his truck no doubt thought it was funny, preoccupied as he was with putting down a hated rival. But the message it conveyed said more about him than he intended, and it cost him that second date.

When someone puts a bumper sticker on their car, it represents just one element of their complex personality; it's one small sample of how they look at the world. Yet to the guy stuck behind them in traffic, it's the defining element of who they are. As a result, the message it sends can cause people to tune them out or write them off. It can even be taken as inflammatory.

Take, for example, the "My Child Is an Honor Student" bumper stickers. That's a nice thought, and Mom probably put it on her minivan out of a combination of delight with and obligation to her wide-eyed fourth grader who proudly brought it home. She displays it to reward her child for hard work, not to brag. But not every other driver interprets it that way—that's why we see stickers that say things like "My Kid Can Beat Up Your Honor Student" or even "My French Bulldog Is Smarter than Your Child." (Yes, that's a real sighting.)

What you say doesn't matter. It's what they hear that counts.

The same is true of branding. It may be OK for you to risk the ire of other drivers by virtue of the stickers you put on your car. But when you're paying big money to develop a brand, the message your audience receives is everything—regardless of what it is you intend to say.

A counselor friend of mine defines communication as "the meeting of meaning." I think that's as good a definition as I've heard. We don't truly communicate simply by saying words; we communicate only if the audience understands what we mean for them to know. The trick to creating effective branding is to walk in the shoes of your target customers, to see your message through their eyes and hear it through their ears.

You might be surprised at how they interpret what you're trying to say. When people hear retailers screaming through the television (as they so often do), "There's never been a better time to buy," they don't think, "There's never been a better time to buy." They think, "There they go again, trying to coerce me into buying a car/sofa/TV." By failing to take into consideration the fact that people may have heard that line once or twice before, brands can be their own worst enemy.

You may like what your brand has to say, but your feelings can be misleading. You, after all, aren't the target. In fact, since you know so much about your products, your industry, your competition, and even your own good intentions, your opinion may be as far from the target audience's as it can get.

Learn the lesson of the bumper sticker. As you study the people you're trying to reach, as you get to know them and understand their attitudes and perceptions, don't just tell them what you want them to know. Reward them for paying attention, make sure you achieve the meeting of meaning, and save self-expression for the back of your car.

13

B2B IS P2P

ONE OF THE REASONS GEICO'S PITCH WORKS IS THAT NOBODY wants to spend more on insurance than they have to. Insurance is a functional thing—a necessity—but the more you spend on it, the less you can spend on the car or the home or the boat or the motorcycle you're trying to protect. Unlike products or services that are fun to buy, we're acutely aware of the trade-offs in buying a necessity like insurance.

The same tends to hold true in business-to-business (B2B) transactions. In fact, because many B2B purchases are complex and carry large price tags, B2B marketers tend to be uncomfortable with even the word "branding."

Not so International Paper (IP). One of the world's largest companies, IP has a hand in manufacturing everything from diapers to greeting cards, office paper to shipping containers, cotton swabs to foodservice packaging. It counts as customers many of the world's biggest consumer brands, but it's not itself a consumer brand.

Once North America's largest landowner, a few years back IP made the strategic decision to divest the majority of its forest resources so it could better serve its customers by focusing on its core manufacturing competencies. Along the way, IP wisely recognized that its brand needed to be transformed as well. IP understood that, as with consumer branding, even the biggest and most complex B2B transactions are made P2P—person to person.

Unfortunately, many B2B brands are their own worst enemies in this regard, in part because of a handful of persistent myths that permeate the industry's thinking. Here are a few.

B2B is different. This is probably the most common misunderstanding—that somehow the rules of branding don't apply in a business-to-business context. Sure, selling to a company is different from selling to a consumer. But it's no more different than selling toothpaste is to selling paint, or even than selling wine is to selling beer. In each case, you're trying to win over a unique group of people who have an existing array of preconceptions and a distinct set of needs. No two branding assignments are alike, yet they're all subject to the same fundamental and unchanging principles.

> **Companies don't buy things. People buy things.**

Information trumps emotion. Anybody who has spent time working in B2B sales and marketing will hear this refrain (or some variation of it): "Make the product the hero," or "Get right to the point," or "Just make sure it has a strong call to action." It's as if the people who read B2B ads don't buy Evian, attend Cirque du Soleil, or shop at Target on the weekends. Or if they do, they somehow disengage the right sides of their brains Monday through Friday.

That's not to say that information isn't important, and especially so when you're dealing with purchases that can run into the thousands or millions of dollars. But the bigger the purchase (typically), the longer the sales cycle. That makes branding even more valuable—and vital. Just because you want your prospects to know something doesn't mean they want to hear it. First you must demonstrate that you understand the challenging world in which your prospects live. Only then perhaps they'll be willing to listen.

Creativity isn't important. This myth is less likely to be articulated but is still widely held. It's why ads in trade magazines tend to be riddled with bullet points. There's nothing wrong with making brand communications for even the most mundane products tasteful and aesthetically appealing. Even people who wear pocket protectors enjoy a good wine, a well-crafted movie, or a beautiful piece of art. To paraphrase ad great David Ogilvy ("The consumer isn't a moron; she is your wife"), the prospect isn't a robot; he is your neighbor.

Companies buy things. I've run my own business for nearly 20 years, and not once has my company bought anything. Companies don't buy things, people do. True, a committee may need to approve the purchase, but even committees are composed of people. And in all but the rarest of cases, there's one person on that committee who holds the key—someone with thoughts and feelings and likes and dislikes and hopes and dreams. Someone who can be captivated and motivated to move your request along.

But what about the "second sale" that's often required in B2B transactions? It's true that once you win one person over, you may still have a lot of work to do. However, this real and challenging complexity doesn't change the fundamental equation. And B2B brands aren't alone in facing it. Ask a breakfast-cereal maker who's more important to win over—Junior or Mom—and the answer you'll get is: "Both." A strong brand can be the best way to win the second sale, particularly if those who are making the call are less involved in the specifics of the transaction.

People are people, and whether they're making a purchase for themselves, their families, their companies, or even their government, their decision-making processes aren't entirely rational. Even when they're thumbing through trade magazines (perhaps especially then), they're attracted to appeals that are unique, interesting, and compelling.

Discard the myths that hold most B2B marketers back, and realize that B2B will always be P2P—person-to-person. You may find that the value of your brand—like IBM, GE, Cisco, and IP—gives consumer brands a run for their money.

14
BRANDS 'R US

STARBUCKS GOT A LOT OF PRESS A FEW YEARS BACK FOR SHUT-
ting down every one of its 7,100 company-owned U.S. stores for two
hours to conduct a "partner" (employee) training event. The event was,
according to a news release, part of the company's ongoing efforts to
"renew its focus on the customer."[1]

Starbucks' bold, store-closing move was about more than training
and free press; it was a potent form of internal branding. Starbucks' cel-
ebrated founder, Howard Schultz, said of the idea: "Our unprecedented
level of commitment to and investment in our people will provide them
with the tools and resources they need to exceed the expectations of our
customers."[2]

Some cynics called it a publicity stunt, but I think it was a sincere
initiative from a company that has long demonstrated a commitment to
both its employees and its customers. Closing the stores sent an unmis-
takable message that Schultz was serious about his expectations that all
135,000 Starbucks employees live the brand.

When Starbucks really began to take off in the mid-1990s, it spent
virtually nothing on marketing. But the company sought and found the
emotional connections surrounding its brand and built upon them everything it became. That's when the brand's internal conception of itself
as "The Third Place" (home, work, Starbucks) was born, summed up
well by an internal manifesto: "Coffee and tea. And hope. And a little
bit of sanity."

The longer I'm in business, the more I've come to believe that companies that overlook internal branding are doing themselves a critical

disservice. Every decision every employee makes has an impact, small or large, on your brand, and what you do internally can bridge the gap between perception and reality, promise and delivery, credibility and hypocrisy. Yet in most companies, internal branding doesn't receive nearly the time, resources, or attention that external efforts do.

Many brands will collect reams of research in an effort to develop intimate portraits of their target audiences. They'll spend big bucks to gain insights into the lifestyles, attitudes, perceptions, needs, and wants that inform their prospects' purchase decisions. Then they'll spend even bigger bucks to leverage that knowledge into external marketing programs to attract an ever-larger number of customers.

> **Your most important target audience is the people who see your brand on their paychecks.**

After all that effort, however, most companies effectively file away all that wonderful information somewhere in the vault of the marketing department. Then they wring their hands when their employees don't deliver as promised.

What if, instead, all of the brilliant insights gained in the external branding process could be ingrained in the minds of each employee? What if there were a deliberate process in place to help employees not only do the functional aspects of their jobs better but also more intimately understand those whom they serve? What if every employee could be enabled and equipped to be a powerful steward of the brand? All of it is possible, and that's why internal branding presents such a big opportunity for improvement in most companies.

Some organizations famously understand this. Disney has long referred to its theme-park employees as "cast members" to ensure that they understand they're always on stage. And there's no more succinct statement of internal purpose than "Semper Fidelis," which the Marine Corps says "is more than a motto—it's a way of life."

When your employees are clear about the company's orientation and intentions, they can address elements of their jobs that are inconsistent or in conflict with those intentions, improving your product or service and creating better customer experiences. And as is the case with Starbucks, Disney, and the Marine Corps, internal branding can also have a positive impact on recruitment and retention, drawing a clearer picture of the type of employees best suited for the organization.

The more you can ensure that the decisions your people make through the course of each day are true to the essence of your brand, the better. Never has it been more true than in today's interconnected world, where running customer commentary on social media sites can have an immediate impact (for good or for ill) on a widespread scale.

If you don't have an effective internal branding program in place, you should think hard about reallocating some of your marketing budget to set one up. Of course, ultimately you have to find a way to fund both internal and external efforts. But if the former is neglected, the latter could end up doing more harm than good.

15

YOUR BRAND IS THEIRS

THE BETTER JOB YOU DO IDENTIFYING AND UNDERSTANDING your "who," the more likely you'll be able to develop a powerful identity. Once you do, you may find yourself facing a whole new challenge: losing control of your brand. What happened to Netflix is a good case in point.

In 1997, a former Peace Corps volunteer and high school math teacher with an advanced degree in artificial intelligence founded a DVD rental-by-mail company. It was a bold move at a time when there was a Blockbuster Video store on every corner and the chain dominated the video rental business.

The move was even more visionary given the name Reed Hastings chose for his start-up: Netflix. Hastings knew that the world was rapidly moving online and that at some point in the future DVDs-by-mail would become flicks-by-net, and he wanted to establish his company for the long term. His foresight paid off, and today Netflix has more than 30 million customers all over the world.[1] (Blockbuster, not recognizing quickly enough where the world was headed, went bankrupt.)

That's not to say that Netflix did everything correctly. In 2011, Hastings decided it was time to split the company in two, change the pricing structure, and unbundle its mail order and online streaming services, renaming the former Qwikster. The idea made sense on paper, since one business was sure to keep growing and one was likely to enter a period of decline. The move would give company management strategic flexibility as circumstances evolved.

There was just one problem. Netflix customers who were shunted into the Qwikster brand resented the idea. They were Netflix fans, after all, and nobody was going to make them Qwikster clubbies without their permission.

As we've seen, a brand is a company's ultimate asset, as unlike physical assets, it can grow in value indefinitely if properly managed. But at the same time, a great brand belongs as much to its customers as it does the company. It's an unusual and delicate partnership.

Think about your favorite brands. They're *your* favorite brands. I've always been a fan of Dr Pepper, and to this day I don't think the brain trust at Dr Pepper fully understands its own brand. I get a little bit offended when I see Dr Pepper's advertising, because in my humble opinion the company has never fully taken advantage of the power of its brand. Or should I say *my* brand.

New Coke was possibly the most pretested new product launch ever, yet it failed in the marketplace. Despite an unprecedented amount of market research, the management team at Coke didn't anticipate the monstrous emotional backlash it would engender by changing the iconic taste. Coke isn't just a particular flavoring of caramel-colored sugar water. Coke is an institution. You don't spend millions of dollars over several decades to establish your product as "The Real Thing" only to abandon it when faced with a challenge, even one as attention-getting and effective as Pepsi's was.

> The more you build brand equity, the less of it you own.

Brands spend so much time and money building equity that rarely do they realize that the stakeholders of that equity are their customers. Management can do what management does, but that won't keep passionate stakeholders who disagree from making their voices heard, which today get quickly and easily amplified.

Sometimes those stakeholders figuratively sell their stock, as many defecting Qwikster-née-Netflix customers did before Hastings reversed course. Sometimes they raise a ruckus, as Coke fans did when the company abandoned its original formula. And sometimes they sit in quiet disappointment, regretting the loosening of the ties that bind them to the brand. The latter condition is the most damaging, as it happens silently.

It can be a bit frustrating to realize that the better job you do in branding, the less your brand belongs to you. But that's the way power branding works. It's no fun to have your best brand advocates take you to task for something they don't like, but tough love is better than no love at all.

WHAT

ONCE YOU KNOW YOUR *WHO,* YOU CAN FOCUS ON YOUR *WHAT.*
What does your brand represent? What drives its value? What sets it
apart? What does it stand for? It's not merely about what you say or even
what you do; it's what you are.

16

BRANDS BELONG

HUMAN BEINGS ARE SOCIAL CREATURES. WE NEED INTERACTION with one another. It's the way we're made. When we meet someone new, we tend either to be drawn to them or to be disinterested for a whole host of reasons (some of which we may not even realize). Over time, however, we develop a continually evolving stable of relationships, some of which last for a lifetime.

That human dynamic is the root of brand loyalty as well. Our "relationships" with brands aren't nearly as deep or meaningful as human relationships, but they do share some of the same characteristics. The extent to which you can create a sense of belonging between your brand and customers is the extent to which you have a powerful brand asset.

We are all members of different clubs. Our neighborhood is a club, our church is a club, and even our place of employment is a club. In some sense we "belong" to each of these clubs by choice—we choose where to live, where to worship, and where to work because we identify with others who do the same in some form or fashion. Many years after I graduated, I was on a business trip several thousand miles from home and spotted a tourist sporting a sweatshirt from my high school all the way across the country. I quite naturally struck up a conversation with her, as we were part of the same club.

Few people have a choice of where they go to high school, but as we get older, our affiliations are increasingly a matter of preference. For example, vehicle brands tend to generate a great sense of belonging. Ever spoken to a Harley-Davidson enthusiast about his loyalty to the brand?

It's powerful. There's even a club—the Harley Owners Group (HOG). You're either in it, or you're very definitely not.

I was reminded of that a few years ago during a first-time visit to a new client. He was (to say the least) a Harley aficionado, his office decked out with brand paraphernalia. It was like being in an office at the local dealership; everywhere I turned I saw another Harley-Davidson logo—on the walls, on the chairs, on the trinkets on the bookshelves, you name it. It was not the typical office of a senior executive at a major corporation. Another time I saw someone wearing a Harley-Davidson T-shirt that said simply "If I have to explain you wouldn't understand." That's belonging.

> **A product is functional; a brand is a friend.**

As with human friends, the brands we adopt as our own give us a sense of comfort, familiarity, and stability; we've come to know and trust them as opposed to the "stranger" that an unfamiliar brand represents.

Friendships that aren't stable aren't really friendships. Sure, all relationships have their ups and downs, but one of the definitions of a true friend is someone you can count on. In the same way, brands that prove themselves faithful over time win our loyalty. Remember the old saying "No one ever got fired for buying IBM"? The truth of that statement was rooted in IBM's reputation for dependability. IBM may have been boring, it may have been expensive, but it was dependable, and that was important.

Sometimes dependability manifests itself in surprising ways. Years ago my wife and I enjoyed a vacation in Jamaica. It's a beautiful island with beautiful people and wonderful food. But if you've ever spent much time in Jamaica, you can get a little tired of allspice, a flavor that dominates much of the cuisine. Imagine my delight on one of our excursions when we spotted a Burger King. I knew that no matter where in the world I was, I could step up to that counter and get a familiar, dependable Whopper.

But here's the thing about dependability. It requires time. As with human relationships, it takes time for brands to develop strong bonds with their customers. Infatuation is exciting (the basis for those late-night infomercials), but it rarely lasts. It turns into either ambivalence or attachment, depending on how well the promise is delivered.

And the time factor is different for different categories. As with human friendship, the more interactions a brand has with its customers, the more the relationship can develop. Particularly for lower-involvement products that people buy infrequently, there can be a big forget factor (just like we forget the name of acquaintances we don't often see).

Not long ago, I heard an ad for an online mortgage brand I once used to refinance my home. Years have passed since I last refinanced and, despite being a satisfied customer, I realized that I had completely forgotten about the brand. The challenge for that company and others like it is to maintain some level of belonging with customers like me (without annoying us, of course).

Brand relationships, like human relationships, need consistent attention and upkeep in order to stay fresh and top of mind. It's not as if they replace or even approach the level of human friendships. But they do add a sense of belonging to our lives.

17
CONSENSUS IS GOOD

JUST GO OUT THERE AND CREATE A BRAND THAT CARRIES A DEEP sense of belonging like Harley-Davidson. Sounds great, doesn't it? Of course it's not that easy. And where to begin might surprise you.

Reams of research have proven that the best brands begin not with a big idea or brilliant strategy. The best brands begin with internal alignment. Great brands are great brands not only in word but also in deed. And that requires clear and long-lasting consensus among the management team (and ideally throughout the organization).

Consensus. Now there's a dirty word. Most businesspeople I know would file that in the lexicon of mismanagement right after "committee" and "compromise." None less than Margaret Thatcher famously said, "Consensus is the absence of leadership."

But consensus gets a bad rap. For her part, Thatcher was referring to defining historical moments in highly charged partisan environments, not the everyday operations of a close-knit team focusing on a strategic objective. While a prime minister (or president, CEO, or manager at any level) needs to be unafraid to make bold decisions, those in his or her charge must operate with clear consensus, or carnage may result. It's as true in the boardroom as it is on the battlefield.

Believe it or not, research demonstrates that something as mundane as a lack of alignment is one of the most common reasons why growth stalls in any company and every industry. Beyond being a common cause, it also may be the most sinister. A lack of consensus is, in theory, controllable. But theory doesn't always line up with reality.

When a company is healthy and growing, sometimes it seems that it can do no wrong. Results are happening as a result of (or perhaps in spite of) its marketing efforts, and nobody's complaining. But at some point, the ground shifts beneath it.

Recession, a disruptive technology, or an aggressive competitor enters the picture, and growth begins to slow. New people the company has added to manage its expansion begin to raise questions. Their opinions, based on differing backgrounds, experiences, and perspectives, confuse the picture. As members of the management team drift along, unable to support a single direction for any length of time, they may blame the economy, the competition, or the person in the office down the hall, without realizing that the problem is more systemic than that.

> **If your brand has veered off course, it may be your team that's in need of an alignment.**

The first step in getting back up to speed is coming to an understanding that the key people on the team all need to be heading in the same direction. Once they are, they can work together to overcome other hindrances to growth. In my firm's two groundbreaking studies of the causes of corporate growth challenges, we found that a lack of consensus among the management team (let alone the rest of the organization) was the leading reason why companies fall off of and can't get back onto the growth curve.[1]

IBM is one of the most valuable—and consistent—brands in the world. It didn't become so by accident. Jon Iwata, the company's SVP of Marketing and Communications, says that IBM's internal corporate values shape everything it does and every choice the management team makes on behalf of the company, including the long-running "Smarter Planet" positioning that has driven much of the growth in IBM's brand value.[2]

The reasons are not so mysterious. Even the best-laid plans won't do a company any good if those charged with executing them are pulling in different directions—or worse, are in open rebellion. Iwata's predecessor, Abby Kohnstamm, underscores the point: "The larger the company, the greater the importance there is to get to a clear, simple brand idea. Ours became a rallying point for the entire organization. It shapes the culture, it shapes business decisions, and it shapes behaviors."[3]

A great deal of research, creativity, and just plain hard work must go into filling the gap between C-level vision and street-level value proposition. That can't even begin to happen if those in the C-suite aren't aligned. But when you can uncover a brand value proposition that both meets a market need and can be aligned all the way up to the corporate vision and mission, you know you're on to something that can drive brand value for years to come.

18
IDEAS ARE IT

WITHOUT INTERNAL CONSENSUS, EVEN THE MOST COMPELLING plans won't get off the ground. But compelling plans are built around compelling ideas, and compelling ideas are the linchpin to effective branding.

Intel is all about performance. The chipmaker is determined to never be outperformed by competing technology on things like speed, energy efficiency, and adaptability. That's why when a computer displays an "Intel Inside" badge, people are more apt to trust it, even if (or perhaps because) they know little about the workings within.

Brands that stand the test of time understand that as valuable as their products and services are, products and services come and go. Brands, however, live on indefinitely. As a result, wise companies invest in and celebrate and protect their brands in every way they can, wrapping them around big, everlasting ideas. Focus is at the root of branding, and what Intel and other dominant companies know is that sustainable success is built on the foundation of a singular idea, around which everything they do is oriented.

Sometimes, as in the case of General Electric, the company is closely associated with an actual word ("Imagination"). In other cases, it's the underlying concept that's important. You won't see Nike highlight the word "motivation" in its advertising, but motivation is what the brand ("Just Do It") is all about. Leading brands like these filter their strategic decisions around their evergreen, animating ideas, which enable them to sustain success over time.

If you can't describe the essence of your brand in a single, simple turn of phrase, it's probably an area in need of improvement. It's easy to poke fun at the thousands of mediocre business books churned out annually. But envisioning a business book—regardless of whether it makes it to store shelves—can be a useful exercise for any brand. The more powerful your brand, the easier it will be to do.

I mentioned *Delivering Happiness,* the book penned by Tony Hsieh, Zappos's popular CEO. Hsieh's unwavering commitment to customer satisfaction made the title of the book almost obvious. Perhaps that's why he was able to sell his then 10-year-old venture to Amazon for about $1 billion.

More than a decade earlier, legendary chief executive Herb Kelleher wrote his own book chronicling the secrets of success at Southwest Airlines. The title was as simple as it gets: *Nuts.* That, in a word, reflected not only Kelleher's easygoing, lighthearted approach to business but the humorous culture and efficiency of his airline.

A handful of other business leaders have had a similar literary vision, possible only because they were so in tune with their brand's reason for being. Loews Hotels' Jonathan Tisch wrote *Chocolates on the Pillow Aren't Enough,* reflecting the company's premise that great products and services need to deliver "experiences that are unique, memorable, and deeply rewarding." Starbucks' Howard Schultz wrote *Pour Your Heart Into It* to share the values by which he built his coffee empire. And Bill Gates's *Business at the Speed of Thought* made the case that a computer on every desk was only the beginning.

If you can't articulate your brand's value proposition, your customers never will.

The discipline of organizing their thoughts into a book compelled each of these business leaders to examine what their companies stood for. And their books reinforced the elements they attributed to their success, which suggests that the volumes belong on the shelves of each of their employees as well as the local Barnes & Noble. A well-written business biography is as much a manual for internal alignment as it is good reading.

GE puts its commitment to imagination this way: "From jet engines to power generation, financial services to water processing, and medical imaging to media content, GE people worldwide are dedicated to turning imaginative ideas into leading products and services that help solve some of the world's toughest problems."[1] As awkward as the company's major initiatives (Ecomagination, Healthymagination) sound, they further reinforce the idea around which the company is based. "What we can imagine," GE says, "we can make happen."[2]

Performance. Imagination. Motivation. These aren't branding ideas; they're business ideas that have branding implications. If you want your branding to be more effective, ensure that it's rooted in the idea that animates your company. If you're not sure what that idea is, it's probably related to why you got into business in the first place. Rediscover your animating idea, make sure it's still sound, and orient everything you do around it—including (but not limited to) your branding messages.

I'm not suggesting that you invest the time in writing a book about your company (at least not yet). Just work on its title. Think of it as an elevator speech for a two-story ride: short and sweet. Avoid the temptation to use clichés that any company could use, such as "Quality Matters" or "Because We Care." Work to come up with something that's clearly distinct.

It might be descriptive like "Delivering Happiness," suggestive like "Chocolates on the Pillow Aren't Enough," metaphorical like "Pour Your Heart Into It," or reflective of your unique attributes and culture, like "Nuts." There's no one way to go about naming a book, and by going through the process of determining the essential idea by which your brand is (or should be) known, you'll gain appreciation for what it's really all about. And you might find it doesn't stand for much, which in itself would be a valuable discovery. Everyone knows you can't judge a book by its cover, but if the title isn't compelling, nobody will ever bother to pick it up.

19

MARGINS TAKE MONEY

IS MICHELIN A BETTER TIRE THAN GOODYEAR? IS BAYER BETTER aspirin than a generic? Is Fiji better water than Dasani? Who really knows?

Sure, each brand has its loyalists, and if you ask the executives at Michelin, Bayer, and Fiji, I suspect they'd have reams of data to prove that their products are the best. But to the average tire, aspirin, or bottled water buyer, Michelin, Bayer, and Fiji aren't demonstrably better than the competition. If you took all the brand indicators off all three products, most people would have no idea which is which.

If that's the case, why are people willing to spend more for products from companies like these? The answer, in a word, is *branding*. These marketers know that the huge investment of time and money they spend on their brands will make their products worth more than similar, lower-priced substitutes. And they're right.

Every product or service has a price/value equation. Its functions, features, attributes, and image add up to a certain value to consumers, who decide—based on a host of reasons—whether or not the total value is worth the price. The more commoditized the product or service, the more pressure the market will bring to bear on pricing.

That's why it's odd that anybody would pay extra for costly tires that the average person couldn't scientifically differentiate from those of a less-expensive brand. Or for branded aspirin, which is, chemically speaking, exactly the same as its unbranded counterpart. Or for water that costs significantly more than the bottle sitting next to it on the supermarket shelf. Yet it happens every day.

There isn't a category of product or service that isn't subject to commoditization pressures. It's easy to wring your hands worrying about pleasing customers on the price side. While many companies host sales, offer discounts, and flood the market with coupons, enlightened brands understand that it's the denominator of the price/value equation that matters. Aggressive competition will always put pressure on pricing; a brand doesn't need to add to that pressure by sending signals that people can (and therefore should) be able to buy it for less.

Margin-driven brands focus on improving the perceptions of their products or services. They add features and benefits, revamp their packaging, and enhance their image by leveraging the principles of power branding. Michelin, Bayer, and Fiji are all premium-priced brands that, logically speaking, shouldn't be able to command a premium. That they are able to do so is an inspiration for us all.

> **In the price/value equation, it's the denominator that counts.**

There are a variety of ways to drive margin through branding—not least, the idea your brand represents and the tone with which it's conveyed. But no brand can get off the ground without a commitment to support it.

Forrest Gump's mother said: "Stupid is as stupid does." In branding, cheap is as cheap does. Regardless of what idea your brand represents, how you present it sends a signal. If you want customers to pay more for your brand, you must believe that it's worthy of your own investment. You might be a great guy, but a T-shirt and flip-flops won't get you a table at 21.

Share of voice is also important. Nielsen Analytic Consulting and the Institute of Practitioners in Advertising studied well over 100 packaged goods brands and found that those whose share of voice exceeded their share of market were better able to catch up with competitors. The study emphasized the importance of the message as well, but it made the point that share gain can happen independent of message content.[1]

This shouldn't come as a surprise. Higher share of voice generates higher levels of awareness and recall, but it also generates confidence.

Consumers intuitively understand that the more a brand spends, the more successful it must be. Brands that advertise more would logically be perceived as more successful than those that advertise less, winning them higher perceived value.

We still don't understand all the ins and outs of why people make seemingly irrational decisions when it comes to the prices they pay. But if you don't invest in your brand, don't expect consumers to. It behooves any company to take a page from the book of successful high-margin brands and spend its resources driving value rather than trimming price. Then don't be surprised when more people begin to agree with your estimation of what your brand is worth.

20

RELEVANCE RULES

THE FACT THAT INVESTMENT DRIVES VALUE IN BRANDING MAKES sense. The more you invest, the greater your return will be. But there's a corollary to that principle: If your "what" isn't highly relevant to your "who," your brand might as well be invisible.

Brands that generate the strongest sense of belonging are so relevant to the wants and needs of their customers that they generate a natural gravitational pull. And they recognize that the wants and needs of those in their "club" change over time.

William Lauder, CEO of cosmetics manufacturer Estée Lauder, says, "The challenge for any brand marketer is how to continue to maintain a modernity or contemporaneous look to your brand while not changing it so much that a loyal consumer says, 'It's not my brand anymore.' It's quite a challenge. Many of the great brands out there have been hurt by being too committed to history and not committed enough to what history offers as an instruction to the future."[1]

Nowhere is that more true than in the automotive industry, where GM, once the largest company in the world, lost its way by losing its relevance with consumers.

GM pioneered the engines that could run on unleaded gas and invented the emissions-reducing catalytic converter. It was even the first company to offer airbags in a production vehicle.[2] But when German and Japanese automakers had a better feel for what ailed Americans during the 1970s energy crisis, GM was slow to respond. Over the next few decades, GM focused on cost savings rather than innovation, and the company's quality and styling fell off. The company famously filed for bankruptcy protection in 2009.[3]

Ford and Chrysler, the other big U.S. automakers, found themselves similarly surprised by their international rivals. But Chrysler, in particular, made an amazing comeback by focusing on relevance. First, then-CEO Lee Iacocca boldly rolled out a new kind of vehicle, the minivan, perfectly timed to coincide with the baby-bearing years of the baby boomers. It was practical, it was fuel-efficient, it fit into a standard garage, it hit a nerve, and it turned Chrysler's fortunes around.

Next came Bob Lutz's turn to lead the company in the 1990s. As I mentioned previously, Lutz knew that market relevance was more important than market size, believing that it was better to be number 1 on the list of a small group of consumers than somewhere down the list for everyone. Under his leadership, Chrysler had such narrowly targeted hits as the Dodge Ram, the Jeep Grand Cherokee, the Chrysler PT Cruiser, and the impractical (but totally cool) Dodge Viper—vehicles that intentionally don't appeal to everyone but were highly relevant to their core target audiences.

> **Relevance is a continually moving target.**

That was several years ago, and unfortunately Chrysler has again been struggling of late, which underscores the point that relevance is a continually moving target. As Mary Wells Lawrence, a member of the Advertising Hall of Fame, put it, "In this business, you can never wash the dinner dishes and say they are done. You have to keep doing them constantly."[4]

Remember the "performance" basis of Intel's brand? For years the key measure of performance was the processing speed of its semiconductors. As chips became more powerful and the devices they were created for more compact, however, the definition of performance had to evolve to encompass other factors, like battery life and heat generation. As the needs of its target market evolve, Intel is evolving with them—but without forsaking its promise of performance.

Gatorade has similarly been able to maintain a commanding market share despite the best efforts of its competitors. The brand was first in its category, relentlessly pursuing its identity as "fuel for athletes," and built a powerful franchise in consumers' minds. But Gatorade has never rested on its laurels and continues to innovate by developing new products that keep its brand relevant in the minds of its core customers.

No one is particularly proud of their high school yearbook photograph. We may have looked pretty fashionable at the time, but fashion is ever changing. Although through the years we remain uniquely ourselves, should the way we relate to the world not continually evolve, we'd all be social rejects.

The same is true of a brand; it must thread the needle between staying consistent and remaining relevant. As long as those responsible for it are willing to figuratively look in the mirror and be honest with themselves, they can ensure their brand stays attractive.

21
SIMPLICITY SELLS

THERE'S A REASON MOST OF THE WORLD'S BEST BRANDS CAN BE characterized by a singular idea. They've reduced their vision and mission to their most fundamental essence, knocking off extraneous complexities, sanding their value proposition down to its essence, and polishing it up. In a word, they've simplified.

One of my favorite all-time commercials is Google's "Parisian Love." Using minimal, almost static shots of a search on the Google home page, in less than a minute the commercial takes us from "study abroad Paris France" through "impress a French girl" and "churches in Paris" to "how to assemble a crib."

It's a charming, theater-of-the-mind love story that celebrates the role Google can play in our lives. That one of the simplest commercials ever was created for a brand that makes its living in the complex world of the web isn't just ironic; it should be encouraging to brands in even the most complicated of industries. The commercial, like the Google home page, is an exercise in simplicity.

No doubt there are many wonderful things about your product or service that you want people to know. If they just knew your brand as well as you do, they couldn't help but become fans. But it's a lot to ask of consumers to allow you to educate them.

New York Times columnist and bestselling author Thomas Friedman says: "There is nothing wrong with complicated ideas, but if you want to convey a complicated thought to a mass audience, you have to first condense it into something digestible and believable. Once you grab someone's attention, you can pour in the details."[1] He may have been referring to his beat of political events and global business trends, but the principle holds true for branding.

There's just too much information out there vying for people's attention these days to expect them to sit still and absorb a complex idea, no matter how true or beneficial it may be. Like it or not, we live in a sound-bite society, and people make judgments quickly. As ad great Bill Bernbach said: "Find the simple story in the product, and present it in an articulate and intelligent, persuasive way."[2] Voltaire was even more succinct: "The best way to be boring is to leave nothing out."[3]

> **Complexity is the enemy of comprehension.**

Subaru has always made good automobiles, with solid engineering, nice styling, and reasonable gas mileage. But a few decades ago, Subaru was about to go extinct in the United States for lack of consumer appeal. The company was saved by focusing on one thing: the beauty of all-wheel drive. It led people who never would have considered a Subaru to give the brand a look, and many of them became brand loyalists. Presenting its story in simple terms invited people in to experience the complexity of the brand.

Subway is another brand that has enjoyed success through simplicity, in its case, meeting the needs of people who reluctantly live a fast-food lifestyle. We all know the story of Jared Fogle, who in 1998 tipped the scales at 425 pounds and decided to go on an all-Subway diet. As he shed some 245 pounds, Jared found a new job as Subway spokesperson, and Subway found a competitive advantage over its less-healthy competitors. And for years the chain has drummed that singular message home in its branding efforts: Eat Fresh.

Millward Brown (the company behind the BrandZ rankings) says Subway is one of two brands that enjoyed four-digit growth in brand value over a seven-year period, and the brand stood out as the "Top Riser" in the 2013 report with a growth in value of more than 5,000 percent. Millward Brown credited Subway's performance to "a great value offer, absolute relevance to consumers, and a genuinely meaningful difference that sets it apart from competitors."[4]

The other brand that enjoyed such a tremendous rise in brand value was, unsurprisingly, Apple. The ever-quotable Steve Jobs once said, "Simple can be harder than complex: You have to work hard to get your thinking clean to make it simple. But it's worth it in the end because once you get there, you can move mountains." The simplicity his company achieved did, in fact, move mountains. Jobs went on to say, "The way we're running the company, the product design, the advertising, it all comes down to this: Let's make it simple. Really simple." And the headline on an old Apple brochure summed it up: "Simplicity is the ultimate sophistication."[5]

Google, Subaru, Subway, and Apple have a lot to offer beyond search, all-wheel drive, eating fresh, and computers. And there is a time and a place for each brand to expand on customers' understanding of their brands. But the way they made a name for themselves was by keeping their pitch simple.

Warren Buffett, the legendary value investor who has made many people rich by cutting through the complexity of the financial markets, may have put it best: "The business schools reward complex behavior more than simple behavior, but simple behavior is more effective."[6]

22
BAD CAN BE GOOD

FOR YEARS LISTERINE, THE LEADING BRAND OF MOUTHWASH, bragged that it was "the taste people hate, twice a day." Power tool manufacturer Stihl made the centerpiece of a long-running campaign the fact that its products can't be found at Lowe's or Home Depot. And a restaurant down the road from me advertises itself as "The World's Worst BBQ." Seems like an odd way to win friends and influence people, doesn't it?

Odd, perhaps. But effective too. All three brands wisely took advantage of a powerful but seldom-used strategy: admitting a negative to get a positive.

This approach dates at least as far back as 1963 when Avis famously coined the slogan "Avis is only No. 2. We try harder." The campaign was revolutionary in its approach because it began with an admission that Avis wasn't the leader in its industry. It was honest. It was daring. And in retrospect, it made perfect sense.

The fact that Avis wasn't number one was obvious to anyone who knew anything about the rental car industry. Avis wasn't revealing any secrets. What it was doing was approaching branding differently from its competitors. And within four years, Avis had tripled its market share.

Despite the success of this type of approach, it is rarely used today—which is one reason why it can still be so effective. Consider the wisdom of Stihl's strategy. Not only did the brand protect its margins by keeping itself from becoming beholden to two very powerful retailers, the fact that its products aren't sold in those stores gives the Stihl brand a cachet that competitors don't have. After all, if Stihl can succeed without the sanction of the world's two largest home-improvement retailers, its products must be good.

The first time I ever heard of Buell motorcycles was via a billboard. The headline said "It's a fast, rude ride. But then again, so is life." I remember being intrigued and impressed that this brand would be so bold. I had been unaware of the nameplate until then, but the line stuck with me. I turned the words over in my mind, wondering what they meant. And I concluded that Buell was a high-performance machine that was not for the average rider—exactly what the brand wanted me to think.

That's the power of admitting a negative. Not only is it different (and therefore refreshing), it causes people to engage with the message. Consumers have become conditioned to discount all the promises, claims, and comparisons most brands make, but that's much harder to do when the claim is self-deprecating. BMW once took out a full-page ad in the *Wall Street Journal* featuring a giant headline that simply said "No." In an industry where getting people to "yes" is the name of the game, that got readers' attention.

If you know it, and they know it, admit it.

It may sound counterintuitive, but admitting a negative builds trust. Nike once ran an ad pointing out how many thousands of free throws Michael Jordan had missed over the years. Wouldn't an athletic company want to boast about how successful its star endorser was rather than how often he had failed? But this ad, like the Avis campaign before it, wasn't revealing any secrets. It was simply pointing out a fact that even the mildest basketball fans already intuitively knew. Admitting it humanized the icon that is Michael Jordan and added depth and richness to the relationship Nike has with its customers.

It may not be right for every situation, but any company, no matter the size, can leverage the principle. Think about what's not so appealing about your brand. Is it small? Big? New? Old? Is it slow? Fattening? Dangerous? Expensive? Is it hard to find? Easy to miss? Whatever it is, chances are people already know it, so there's really very little risk in admitting it.

Consider turning your big negative into a hook. Then use that hook to draw prospects into the rest of the story. If it's done correctly, you'll not only get their attention, you'll also gain their trust. And you'll leave your competitors scratching their heads. Which is never a bad thing.

23
DIFFERENT IS REFRESHING

BEFORE HE WAS AN ACADEMY AWARD–WINNING ACTOR, MORGAN Freeman starred in a commercial in which he explained to his coworker why he continues to use Listerine despite its terrible taste. He says he's tried others but since they don't taste as bad, they must not kill the germs that cause bad breath as well. The commercial ends with that infamous tagline, "The taste people hate, twice a day."[1]

Not only is this a great example of the principle that bad can be good, it demonstrates how refreshing different can be. Listerine was the only breath freshener that had the guts to boast of bad taste. That got people's attention in the breath freshener category, one that's as commoditized as any. Beyond mouthwashes like Listerine and Scope you've got lozenges like Certs and Tic Tac, gums including Trident and Dentyne, and now spritzers and strips of all stripes promising to clean your teeth, freshen your breath, or make you more popular. Not an easy category in which to compete, unless you want to spend millions and millions of dollars shouting down your competition.

What to do? Listerine's boast, brilliant as it was, works only for Listerine. But Listerine's strategy will work for any brand. The best way to compete—in breath freshening or any other category—is to focus on being not better but different.

That's how Altoids became Altoids. Originally created in Europe in 1780 to relieve intestinal discomfort, the brand made its way to America in 1918 and shortly thereafter was promoted as an antidote to poisons in the stomach. That was the genesis of a big—and lasting—brand idea: The Curiously Strong Mint.[2]

It's a positioning that has remained relevant through changing times, in part driven by Altoids' willingness to develop "curiously strong" quirky-bordering-on-offensive ads. When it comes to halitosis, there's bad breath and then there's baaaad breath. When you need something strong, think Altoids.

A brand can differentiate based on any number of things, from features to packaging to price. Maker's Mark doesn't brag about great taste; instead, it wants you to know that its bourbon "is handmade every step of the way." Absolut became one of the most famous branding case studies ever by celebrating the shape of its vodka bottle. And Target achieved what *Advertising Age* called "the ultimate retail positioning" by crafting an image that transcends simple description (although '*Tar-zhay*' is pretty good shorthand for it).[3]

Here's a technique that any brand can use to develop a number of potential points of differentiation: the Five S's. Is there *someone* your brand serves better than others (Mountain Dew)? *Something* that makes it unique (Altoids)? *Somehow* about the way it's made (Maker's Mark)? *Sometime* that it's best used ("Weekends were made for Michelob")? *Somewhere* it's perfect for (Tide to Go)? Spend a few hours brainstorming answers to these questions for your brand, and you're likely to come up with a dozen or more potential points of differentiation.

There's no competition in a category of one.

Keep in mind that whatever claim you stake has to be consistently delivered on or it will flop, no matter how strong the idea. I once stayed at a big hotel chain that trumpeted its slogan with great pride: "Be Hospitable." Yet when I called the front desk to request a late checkout because of a meeting I was attending in the hotel's conference center, I had to argue with the clerk to get just one additional hour. What do you think I'm going to remember every time I see the company's ads? An empty promise.

Which takes us back to internal alignment. The more narrow your target, the more narrowly differentiated your brand, the more internally aligned you are around it, the more it will offer real, lasting return. Kind of like the fresh breath that comes from a curiously strong mint.

24
FEELINGS COME FIRST

TRAVELING IS HARD. BEING AWAY FROM HOME, EATING OUT, sleeping in an unfamiliar bed—not to mention the nightmares of airports and airlines—make even the most hardened road warrior appreciate small niceties.

It was one of those niceties that brightened my life one day back in 2003. I was attending a conference at a resort in Palm Springs, and I rolled out of bed before dawn to get to an early seminar. I shuffled my sleepy feet into the bathroom and turned on the water. Stepping into the shower, I tugged on the curtain. To my surprise (and delight), there was no vacuum of air sucking in the unruly vinyl and trapping me against the wall. In fact, the reason I noticed the curtain at all was that it was standing completely still.

Wondering what this was all about, I looked up and saw what struck me as one of the most wonderful inventions of all time: a curved shower-curtain rod. What a brilliant concept, I thought. How simple. How obvious. How come nobody ever thought of this before? I was happy. And grateful, not only to the inspired inventor who came up with the concept but also to the hotel that was thoughtful enough to install it.

Now here's the bad news. I don't remember where I was staying. This terrific invention, this fabulous innovation, this morning-making milestone that could have made the difference next time I booked a room didn't have a lasting impact. Other hotels immediately started adopting the feature, and I lost track of who was first. The curved shower-curtain rod was great news for the frequent traveler but provided no lasting differentiation for any one brand. My kids will have no memory of life without it.

That's the problem with product and service improvements. Curved rods, rearview cameras, artificial sweeteners, camera phones—all are nice, but none offers sustainable differentiation. Sure, they can offer tactical advantages for a period of time, but like any successful innovations, they will be duplicated. Even if they're patented, they'll likely be ripped off by crafty imitations.

So what's a brand to do? How can it achieve differentiation that is real, meaningful, and sustainable? The answer doesn't always lie in left-brain benefits; there's a whole world of right-brain connections that can be tapped. Successful differentiation can take place not only in the minds of customers but in their hearts as well.

That's how Doubletree has made its brand stand out in the bitterly competitive hotel industry. For more than two decades, Doubletree has been giving away its trademark chocolate-chip cookies. Like any hotel chain, Doubletree focuses on many different ways of making its guests comfortable, but more than 21 million times each year, its customers sink their teeth into warm, moist, signature cookies.[1]

Sure, most hotels will offer some sort of sweet snack, but nothing like Doubletree's. Ask the average business traveler what differentiates most hotels, and you'll get a host of random answers. Ask them what differentiates Doubletree, and you'll get one answer—usually accompanied by a smile. Research now shows there's science behind it—the scent of baked goods actually boosts kindness and stimulates good feelings.

Win the heart and the mind will follow.

Or consider the Mini Cooper. How did this funny-looking upstart break out in the übercompetitive automotive market, especially with its tiny (by comparison) marketing budget?

Sure, the car has some impressive features, but features alone don't differentiate. The marketers behind the Mini smartly realized that the key was to find an emotional nook for the brand—and to occupy that nook with every marketing dollar, from a publicity stunt that featured a

Mini catching a piggyback ride on top of a Chevy Suburban (more on that later) to advertising that attached a life-size model of the car to a billboard.

These brands' strategies reflect an understanding that when it comes to brand identity, the whole is greater than the sum of its parts. As we've seen, brands that exist in categories with the most parity (cars, soft drinks, cosmetics, fashion) understand that since their rational benefits are so close to what competitors offer, emotional differentiation can make the difference. That's how Coke and Pepsi justify hiring seven-figure celebrity spokespeople, hoping the emotional connection consumers have with the stars rubs off on their products.

One obstacle you may have to deal with as you pursue emotional differentiation is the left-brain type within your organization who simply doesn't understand the realities of consumer behavior (there's that internal alignment thing again). He thinks a brand's appeal can be boiled down to formulas and arguments—often making his case wearing designer clothes and sipping bottled water, oblivious to the irony.

People buy products and services for a whole host of reasons—some of them rational, some emotional. In well-established categories where a great deal of rational explanation is unnecessary, likability becomes all the more important. To the extent that your emotional differentiation rewards people (the smell of a freshly baked cookie, the sound of a finely tuned engine), it will build affection in their minds. And that affection will pay off in increased trial and brand loyalty.

If a competitor of yours has carved out a sustainable niche, don't attack its strength. Study how it was done, recognize the underlying principles, and apply those principles to your unique set of circumstances. Don't try to mimic Mini's idea of fun or take a bite out of Doubletree's cookie; find your own emotional corner of the world and own it. The deeper you go with it, the more differentiated—and sustainable—your brand will be.

25
CONVENTIONS CAN
BE CHALLENGED

INDUSTRIES OF ALL STRIPES CAN GET SO INBRED THAT IT'S DIF-ficult for any one player to break out from a branding standpoint. Too often, brands focus on what others in their category are doing and end up fighting over the same mental turf. That's a shame, because recognizing—and challenging—industry or marketplace conventions is a great way to stand out.

One of the best Super Bowl commercials of all time challenged the convention that big-game ads had to be big-budget extravaganzas. E*TRADE's simple spot featuring a monkey dancing on a trash can was about as low budget as a commercial can get. But its tongue-in-cheek, self-referential punch line, "Well, we just wasted $2 million bucks. What are you doing with your money?" hit a sweet spot and helped make E*TRADE a household name.

Who would have thought that an ad for an investment brokerage would be more beloved than ads for beer and chips that tend to dominate the Super Bowl? Then again, it wasn't long ago that insurance commercials were as dull and boring as most financial industry ads. We've already given GEICO its props, but the brand deserves another mention for breaking the mold of its own industry conventions.

Rather than mimicking the serious-minded pleas from the likes of "Good Neighbors" and "Good Hands People," GEICO introduced us to a wisecracking gecko, an insecure caveman, an insincere congressman, and other inventive ways of interpreting its low-price/no-hassles message. The AFLAC duck was hatched around the same time, and since then one insurance company after another has headed down the humor road, beginning with smaller players like Nationwide and Progressive and ultimately including old stalwarts like Farmers, State Farm, and Allstate (which took the form to new heights—or depths, judging from the initial criticism—with its "Mayhem" character, who personalizes and pokes fun at serious mishaps. Nothing quiets criticism like success, however, and the Mayhem campaign by all accounts quieted its critics.)

Does that mean that humor is the new convention in the insurance industry, ready to be broken? Perhaps. But all business is an endless cycle of innovation and commoditization. New inventions, ideas, or ways of communicating move the world forward, only to be soon imitated by competitors. What were once breakthrough ideas can become new industry conventions, and the cycle begins anew.

Everybody knew you had to meet face-to-face with an attorney until LegalZoom said you didn't. Or that used car buying involved shady dealers and price haggling until CarMax offered an alternative. Or that self-service yogurt bars couldn't work until Menchie's proved they could. I even remember the old days, when the thought of a bank in a grocery store was unheard of, paying a subscription fee to watch TV was laughable, and there would never be any such thing as a national newspaper.

The way it has always been done is not the way it must always be done.

You can identify endless sources of differentiation by simply taking a step back and honestly examining the conventions of your industry. Is everybody competing to offer the lowest price? Consider how you might charge a premium. Is a wide selection a prerequisite? Try going narrow. Look for opportunities to push when your competitors pull or spring forward when they fall back. You get the idea.

No matter what business you're in, everything you do can be done differently. Doesn't it make sense to challenge your own conventions before someone else does? Spend some time identifying every industry convention you can—product features, service dimensions, price points, distribution methods, marketing messages, media tactics, you name it. Then have some fun imagining approaches that counter each one.

You're sure to discover that a lot of your ideas are nonstarters, but you're just as likely to find a pony in there somewhere. As long as you don't compromise your core competency—the peace of mind insurance brings, the liquid assets people expect from a bank, the confidence athletes need in their athletic apparel—you may be surprised by how many things your industry takes for granted that are based on outdated assumptions and conventions.

Be open-minded, and you might just come up with the next great breakthrough. It won't keep you in the lead forever (success always breeds mimicry), but it will give you a better view than the guy on your tail.

26
COUNTERBRANDING WORKS

E*TRADE MADE A NAME FOR ITSELF BY CHALLENGING THE CON-
ventions of Super Bowl advertising. The Puppy Bowl did so by challenging the Super Bowl itself.

For years Animal Planet has run "the biggest event on all fours," in
which cute, cuddly puppies "mix it up on the grand gridiron of Animal
Planet Stadium" in the same time slot as the biggest sporting event of
them all.[1] It's a classic case of counterprogramming, as Animal Planet
pursues those (few) television watchers who couldn't care less who wins
the football game.

Counterprogramming is an age-old strategy used by television networks, radio stations, and movie studios to attract audiences for whom
their competitors' offerings may not be so appealing. It's the reason why
in past years we've witnessed NASCAR events and children's movies
opposite the Academy Awards and cheap art-house films premiering
the same week as big-budget special effects extravaganzas.

Even the most popular programs and products don't appeal to everyone. Being boldly different—what we might call counterbranding—
can really make a brand stand out.

Quick-service restaurants have been on the defensive for years. It
began when increasing numbers of health-conscious consumers began
questioning the high calorie count and questionable nutritional value
of the typical fast-food meal. It gathered momentum with high-profile
criticism from consumer advocacy groups and documentaries beginning
with Morgan Spurlock's health-horror flick, *Super Size Me*. Clearly, the

trend is not working in the fast-feeders' favor, and industry leaders such as McDonald's and Taco Bell have since introduced healthier fare.

Not Carl's Jr. The chain proudly touts products like a 730-calorie, 47-fat-grams Monster Biscuit and its Jim Beam Bourbon Six Dollar Burger, packed with 960 calories and 48 grams of fat.[2] For several years Carl's Jr. has defied industry trends by touting the size and sloppiness of its sandwiches. Even its signature line of Six Dollar Burgers don't cost $6; they were named to draw a parallel with the more expensive burgers you'll find at a casual dining restaurant. That in itself is a bold naming convention that reflects Carl's Jr.'s bold branding strategy.

While competitors pursue a growing segment of nutrition-conscious consumers, Carl's Jr. shamelessly serves fast food's heaviest users (no pun intended): hungry, invincible young men for whom quantity matters as much as quality. The brand's counterbranding approach has enabled it to stand out in a crowded fast food field.

> **If you want to get noticed, stand apart from the crowd.**

Southwest Airlines also has counterbranding in its DNA, long bucking industry conventions like in-flight meals (peanuts, anyone?), assigned seating, and the hub-and-spoke approach most airlines use to move people across the country. Southwest has responded to decisions, by its competitors to nickel-and-dime their passengers, boldly stating "Fees Don't Fly with Us." Southwest doesn't charge fees for baggage, snacks, window seats, pillows, blankets, water, or even fuel (easy to get away with when you call the fee a "surcharge").

Keep in mind that Southwest would make hundreds of millions of dollars if it quietly followed its competitors' desperate tactics, and with the equity it has built up over the years, it could probably fly somewhat under the radar in doing so. But instead the company has taken the opportunity to reinforce its brand idea in a public—and proud—way. It's a perfect example of effective counterbranding.

Taking a countercompetitive (and sometimes even counterintuitive) approach can be a great way to get people's attention and make your brand stand out. Put more product in your packages, not less. Sell a narrower selection, not a broader one. Be intolerant about something (just not a social or political issue). When all of your competitors are headed down the same road, take one less traveled. That may turn some people off, but it will fire others up.

27
SCARCITY DRIVES VALUE

IF DIAMONDS WERE A DIME A DOZEN, YOU COULD BUY A DOZEN diamonds for a dime. The reason you can't is that diamonds are hard to come by. Whether it's because high-quality diamonds are rare finds or because the diamond industry has done a good job manipulating supply (there is some debate about this[1]), to the average person, diamonds are scarce. As with classic cars, comic books, and bird's nest soup, scarcity drives value.

Have you ever had an In-N-Out burger? It's fast food, but it's not particularly fast, the menu is notable for its lack of variety, and the stores look like they're right out of the 1950s. Founded in 1948, it took the brand nearly 60 years to grow to 200 locations, and only recently has the company opened its first stores in Texas, which is as far east as it gets. But everywhere you find an In-N-Out, you'll find a line out the door. It's a classic cult brand that even has a secret menu that only customers "in the know" know.

It's unusual for a brand to pursue a scarcity strategy, given that we're conditioned to want as many people as possible to have access to our products and services. But In-N-Out understands that it can handle growth only at a certain pace, so it makes sense to stage that growth in such as way as to leverage the power of scarcity.

This point came rushing back to me the other day when I heard a radio commercial for an electronics retailer in which the company boasted about how small its selection of HDTVs was. The spot wasn't apologizing for the lack of selection, nor was it saying the fact that the store carried fewer options than the competition didn't matter. The commercial actually touted the fact that this retail brand had improved the HDTV buying process by limiting its selection to only the most popular models (music to my ears, given my previous television shopping experience).

What this retailer did may have been odd, but it was right on the mark. Conventional wisdom suggests that having more HDTV options under one roof is better for consumers. After all, if a store carries all of the options, it's more likely to be able to meet the needs of every customer who walks through the door. That's the theory, at least.

What this brand recognized, however, is that most people's purchasing needs aren't merely tied to product features. Early adopters aside, most people do not need to spend hour after hour sorting through product reviews and comparison charts to find out which model is best. Most need to know that when they plunk down one, two, three, or more thousand dollars, they're going to be happy with their purchase. And they need to know that in two years they won't be stuck with obsolete technology. (Betamax, anyone?) If they can go to a trusted store and choose from a handful of models that will do the job just fine for the average person, they will be happier than if they are required to sort through dozens of options.

The harder something is to get, the more people want it.

Think about how quickly technology is changing, how rapidly new innovations get introduced to the marketplace, and how many new concepts we are exposed to day after day. It's a crazy thought, but our ability to invent new products has perhaps surpassed our ability to absorb them. We simply can't keep up. In this environment, companies that can find ways to simplify consumer decision making by limiting our choices may find a new competitive advantage.

There's a reason why all of the big fast-food chains now feature a handful of combo meals on their menu—they're more profitable for them, to be sure, but they also make their customers' lives just a little bit simpler. That's a lesson In-N-Out Burger understood from the beginning.

Scarce isn't always bad. More isn't always better. Too many choices are often too confusing, and too much selection can become a burden, not a benefit. As with many good things in life, showing some restraint is not a bad idea.

28
COPYCATS NEVER CEASE

IT'S A CLASSIC STORY THAT REPEATS ITSELF OVER AND OVER IN business: A company pioneers a new product or service. The brand grows fast. Its growth attracts competitors. Differentiation gets hazier, margins suffer, and, often, growth stalls. Low barriers to entry only exacerbate the problem.

In research my firm conducted among hundreds of the fastest-growing companies in the United States, nearly 60 percent of them were the pioneers in their niche. That means that at one time they had 100 percent market share. But by the time we interviewed them, the average company had a market share of less than 16 percent and market rank of number three. What happened?

Competition happened. The more success a brand experiences, the more it will spawn copycats and clones—companies seeking to duplicate its technology, mimic its business model, or imitate its appeal. Underestimating aggressive competitors that want what you've got is a common pothole that trips up less vigilant brands.

A century ago, Coca-Cola stood in a category by itself. But competitors entered the category, blurred the distinctions, and brought on a whole new set of challenges. Yet today, Coke remains one of the world's most valuable brands because the company understands that the product itself is only one aspect of its brand idea.

In our research, we found that most struggling brands became victims to aggressive competitors because they failed to maintain an adequate degree of differentiation. Differentiation enhances perceived value because it creates that wonderful condition, scarcity. When the market offers too many acceptable alternatives to a particular product or service, perceived value declines.

The more success you have, the more your competitors will try to claim the ground you've staked. There was a time when CNN was the only cable news network, and it developed a loyal following that kept it on top for years. But its success attracted copycats, and now CNN has lost its leadership position. Miller Lite was the first beer to combine "tastes great" and "less filling." But today there are dozens of light beers, and Miller Lite is struggling to find its place.

You may think that staying out in front of aggressive competitors means outspending them. That's one way of doing it, but there are other, smarter ways to own and protect your niche. In our study, fewer than 25 percent of the companies that managed to maintain strong growth did so by spending more money than the competition. Instead, they outsmarted them, keeping close tabs on competitive moves while increasing the sophistication of their own branding efforts.

> **When you set the pace, you're the one they chase.**

Brands that have managed to achieve success over the long term understand that, as markets mature, differences blur. They know that their challenge is not to be better than the competition but to stay different.

Sure, Coke has a secret formula that it keeps locked up in its Atlanta vault. But beyond its syrup, Coke knows that its brand is based on far more than just the product but also on its packaging, pricing, distribution, advertising—everything that the company is and does. Coke remains valuable because only Coca-Cola is *Coca-Cola* (a lesson it was reminded of the hard way by the New Coke debacle). Its success is due less to the secrecy of its recipe than the sophistication of its branding.

Whether a company is young or old, public or private, the challenges of competition stay the same. The more success you attain, the more quickly and aggressively competitors will invade your turf. You have to stay one step ahead of them.

29
INNOVATION PREVENTS LIQUIDATION

MAINTAINING RELEVANT DIFFERENTIATION IS ESSENTIAL TO EVERY brand. As long as competition thrives and technology continues its relentless march forward, brands that don't evolve are destined for extinction.

The good news is that remaining relevant doesn't always require radical innovation. That's what's so impressive about the brilliant simplicity of Amazon's shipping program, Amazon Prime.

For a company that ships 100 percent of its products, finding a way to neutralize pressure on shipping costs is no small thing—especially when it's competing with Walmart, which offers its online customers 97-cent shipping on many products or the option to pick up their orders at a nearby store for free.

Millions of Amazon Prime members pay an annual fee for automatic two-day shipping on all of their purchases. Not surprisingly, they tend to be Amazon's most frequent customers, which means they're still getting a pretty good deal. But the program helps ensure they'll turn to Amazon first when they have a new purchase occasion, and the numbers indicate they increase their spending with the company some 20 percent after signing up.[1]

Just goes to show you that innovation isn't the exclusive purview of high-tech R&D departments. While many online retailers have thrown in the towel on shipping charges, Amazon found a way to offset them while increasing order flow. The company took one of its biggest lemons and turned it into a refreshing beverage for its most frequent customers.

Which brings up an important point. Any discussion of innovation presupposes an audience that innovation will benefit. As with Amazon, a great place to begin is with your most loyal customers. Not only do you have a relationship with those customers, but it's a lot cheaper to keep them on board than it is to win new ones. In addition, the more relevant you remain to your best customers, the more likely you are to attract people like them. And since you already are familiar with them, you have a good opportunity to understand their evolving needs.

Keep in mind that there's a difference between knowing facts about your customers (names, zip codes, household income, purchase history, etc.) and truly knowing them. Step one in a continuous innovation program is to put in place an ongoing consumer discovery process.

Continually learn as much as you possibly can about your customers— not just what makes them happy, but what frustrates and disappoints them as well. Ask them what hassles and inconveniences surround the occasions when they do business with you. Find out what alternative solutions they may consider, what substitutes they sometimes choose, and what they do (and why) before and after they transact business with you.

You can gather this insight through formal research methods or by informally observing, listening to, and having conversations with your customers. While they may take the initiative to suggest product or service enhancements, you can't depend on customer ideas alone to keep your company relevant. As we've seen, customers aren't likely to have a sense of the newest developments within your industry or to understand the technical details behind what's possible. Nor are they likely to care as much as you do about the health of your company. Very few products or services are irreplaceable, and your customers have a lot more important things to worry about.

Look for things that aren't working for them. The better you understand the pain points within and around your industry, the better you can enhance your brand's relevance. Run-flat tires reduce the inconvenience (and danger) people feel when they run over a nail. Satellite radio eliminates the annoyance of static on lonely interstate highways. The Egg McMuffin lessens the hassle of eating in the car. Even minor enhancements can have a major impact on customer satisfaction, from my beloved curved shower curtain rod to a web form that remembers personal data (key in my address? again?) to a safe apple slicer (great for you and me, even if it's not so good for Band-Aid).

Once you have a solid list of pain points, consider how you might relieve them. This is where understanding the changing lifestyles of your target prospects is vital, as it gives you a sense of what they'll be wanting/needing/expecting down the road. Some new ideas may require a costly and significant overhaul of the way you do business, while others will require only a simple process change, ordering option, or service enhancement. Over time, you'll probably implement a variety of ideas encompassing all of the above.

> **You can't see around the corner from the comfort of your couch.**

Need a head start? Try imagining solutions from the perspective of well-known, well-respected brands. For each pain point, ask: "How would Nordstrom overcome this problem if it was in our business?" "How would Southwest Airlines approach this challenge?" "What would the Marines Corps do about this issue?" Ritz-Carlton, Harley-Davidson, the Mayo Clinic—you can drop any number of brands into this equation that will cause you to consider different ways of relieving the pain. Many of your ideas won't be practical (and some may not even be possible), but the exercise will open your mind to creative solutions.

And here's a freaky thought: According to Cisco Systems, only 1 percent of every physical touchpoint that can be digitally connected has been connected.[2] What kind of innovation possibilities open up for your brand when the other 99 percent can talk to each other?

Regardless of how you go about innovating, make sure you're continually pursuing the next thing, because a company's commitment to staying relevant must never cease. As you consistently address your customers' evolving expectations and overcome the things that frustrate them, improvements that by themselves may be measured only in inches will move your company miles ahead of where it is today. That's where your customers will be, and as long as you're there to meet them, they're likely to stay with you.

30

FORM CAN TOP FUNCTION

ONE FORM OF INNOVATION THAT'S OFTEN OVERLOOKED IS DESIGN innovation. How things look and feel can be as important as what they do, and focusing only on functionality is to miss significant opportunities for improvement.

For example, I don't know about you, but I've never met anyone who loves the Facebook user interface. It's not exactly Bauhaus style (although I did discover a Bauhaus fan page on Facebook). Twitter isn't exactly a thing of beauty, nor is Google+. But it's not surprising that Facebook and its social media brethren haven't yet achieved the design prowess of Apple, Herman Miller, or Bang & Olufsen. They're just too new to this world.

In every category of industry, form tends to follow function. When Henry Ford was around, cars were clunky, functional things. He is famous for having quipped that customers could have any color they wanted, "as long as it's black." Since then, car design has come a long way; once the wrinkles of the internal combustion engine and suspension, cooling, and safety systems (among many other things) began to be ironed out, attention could be turned to color, styling, and ergonomic issues.

More recently, the first personal computers were clunky to look at, never mind to use. Now they're fashion statements. Office furniture, running shoes, smartphones, you name it—out of the gate, new products appeal based on what they do, but the key to longevity becomes how they do it.

Form follows function in services as well. One of the things I so appreciate about my accounting firm is that it makes the complex simple.

Obviously, the most important service any accounting firm provides is helping clients navigate the byzantine U.S. federal tax code. But my firm takes it a step further, providing me a tax packet with clear instructions about what I'm to sign, how much I need to pay (both annually and quarterly) by when, with preprinted payment slips attached to envelopes already addressed to the proper federal and state government offices. All I have to do is sign, seal, stamp, and send. What is for the accounting firm a simple extra step in the service delivery process is for me a real time-saver and headache-reducer. It only increases my confidence in their capabilities.

The accounting industry, like the automotive industry, the computer industry, and most others that have been around for a while, has had time to muse on how form can augment function. So perhaps we should cut those disorienting social media platforms some slack. Because they're still in their first generation, they simply haven't fully awakened to the benefits of better form.

Has your brand? It's easy to limit your conception of branding to ads, news releases, Web sites, e-mails, trade shows, and the like. But as we've discussed, there isn't anything you do in the delivery of your product or service that doesn't communicate something, intentionally or not. Any brand can improve its form factor, given the proper mindset.

The most important consideration is to ensure that the way you do what you do isn't working against you. Your primary adversary is the mirror image of your brand's core competency—what you might call its evil twin. The first step is to quit being your own worst enemy.

If you run a law firm, for example, the last thing you want to be associated with is unprofessionalism. Are your attorneys hard to get a hold of? Are your invoices confusing? Do your associates play a game of musical chairs on key client accounts? None of these things may bear directly on the quality of your legal advice, but together they sure sap confidence.

Or perhaps you're in retail, where anything that makes it more difficult for people to buy is the enemy. That includes not only the obvious things like running out of inventory or being short-staffed but disconcerting sensory signals like bad lighting, out-of-date décor, odd odors, too much noise (or perhaps too little), or a parking lot in need of striping.

You get the idea. Job #1 must be to stamp out anything that works against your brand throughout the continuum of customer experience. Then, once your defense is in place, you can start tossing the ball around on offense.

> **Substance and style are not mutually exclusive.**

Say you're a restaurateur, for example. First, disarm your evil twin by eliminating anything that conveys bad taste (literally or figuratively), from dirty restrooms to surly staff to sticky menus. Then turn your attention to how you might use form to generate real business results.

Dessert is a source of undertapped margin for most restaurants. It's easy for customers to say no to the same old apple pie pitch, even if it is a generations-old family recipe. But vary the form of the dessert sales experience—walking a piping hot, aromatic pie past the table at just the right time, offering bite-size portions instead of diet-buster slices, developing a tantalizing script to help the wait staff romance the sale—and watch the pie fly. The product itself might remain unchanged, but its form—the way it's presented and positioned—can be renewed continually.

Here's the point: Don't get stuck in a "branding is a department" mindset. There's nothing you do that isn't sending a message, one way or another. Even if you're the most industrial of industrial manufacturers, don't ignore the power of aesthetics and ergonomics. All other things being equal, pretty beats ugly every time.

Think "form" across the entire enterprise, and you'll continually find opportunities for improvement for your business—and your brand.

HOW

IF YOU KNOW WHO, AND YOU KNOW WHAT, YOU'RE ALREADY ahead of the curve. But be careful—the next step is to consider how, and this is where many brands get tripped up. Be signal, not noise.

31
FIRST IMPRESSIONS MATTER

HAVE YOU HEARD OF THE TERM "SPEED DATING"? IT'S A TIME-saver for lonely singles in major metropolitan areas. A host of entrepreneurs have risen up to take advantage of the craze, forming companies with descriptive names such as 8 Minute Dating, HurryDate, and Pre-Dating.

According to Pre-Dating, speed dating "is a fun, safe and efficient way for busy single professionals to meet in person. You'll meet other people in your age and interest group through a series of face-to-face six minute 'pre-dates' in a private area at a local upscale restaurant/bar. Wow . . . many face-to-face 'dates' in just 1 night!!"[1]

Wow indeed. Make a good impression in those first six minutes, or the "relationship" is over. That's a lot of pressure. Believe it or not, even six minutes may be too many by a factor of two. According to communications professor Michael Sunnafrank, people tend to draw conclusions about someone within as little as three minutes of having met them.[2] And researchers at Carleton University suggest that it takes as little as $1/20$th of a second for people to register likes and dislikes about another person.[3] That's fast.

Of course, there can be significant debate about whether this is a good thing. We've all drawn conclusions about others based on first impressions that were later proven incorrect. And it's not hard to find stories about people who made impulsive decisions based on "love at first sight" and later regret it. (Perhaps they should have given it more than $1/20$th of a second.)

But whether someone should act on first impressions or not doesn't change the fact that first impressions exist—and they're powerful. And it's just as true in branding as it is in human relationships.

Unfortunately, many brands don't seem to recognize this. They're like the guy who goes on a speed date and expects to get engaged in six minutes. Not only will it not happen, but by coming on too strong, he'll ruin his chances for even a second date. To put it in business terms, it's extremely rare that you'll be able to open and close the sale all in one meeting.

A great branding plan includes a mix of tactics all designed with a specific purpose in mind. Some approaches are meant simply to make a good first impression, some to provide more information, and some to ask for the order. But the process has to unfold in a time and manner with which the target feels comfortable.

If your brand comes on too strong at first, it may not get a second chance.

Tiffany has been an advertiser in the *New York Times* since the 1920s, and over the years it has come to own a "franchise" four-inch-by-seven-inch position on page 3. Sure, it usually features a product in the ad, but it's more of a tradition than it is a hard sale. Tiffany has an image to uphold, and it does so all the way through the sales process.

Consider the company's Web site. Caroline Naggiar, Tiffany's senior vice president of marketing, says, "Most Web sites are like the front page of a supermarket tabloid—50 things going at once with the bells ringing. Tiffany is not about being fast and expedient . . . we're about graceful behavior, and beauty and quality. The site was an enormous exercise in being reserved, in pulling back. We wanted to be an oasis."[4]

There's a time to open the sale, a time to foster relationship, and a time to ask for the order. Great brands understand this and don't expect every ad to perform every function. In fact, the best brands focus most of their energy on fostering the relationship, believing that prospective customers with whom they engage will want to spend their time and money with them. Sounds like a great dating strategy.

Pay attention to the first impressions your branding efforts are making. Don't ask them to do too much. Consider a little subtlety. And by all means take a step back and evaluate the messages you're sending at each stage of the process.

Don't be like my now-former brokerage firm, which announced its new name with a brochure boasting "A shorter name, the same unparalleled capabilities." It should have been more careful not to include the brochure in the same envelope as an account statement showing the value of my portfolio cratering. Those were "unparalleled capabilities" I didn't need.

32

SLOGANS ARE OVERRATED

A FEW YEARS AGO, THE EDITORS OF *ADVERTISING AGE* CAME UP with a ranking of the top slogans of the twentieth century. At the top of the list: "Diamonds are forever," for DeBeers. The turn of phrase perfectly juxtaposed the long-lasting luster of a diamond with the love that it so often signifies. It was the ideal ribbon around the package of a powerful brand.

Other slogans that made the all-century list included Maxwell House's "Good to the last drop," Miller Lite's "Tastes great, less filling," and Morton Salt's "When it rains, it pours."[1] These verbal icons are likely to be recognized by almost everyone over the age of 30.

Today, however, memorable slogans are the exception, not the rule. Take a brief test yourself. Coca-Cola may be "The real thing," but you probably aren't aware of its current slogan. How about IBM? Google? Microsoft? Samsung? Toyota? Despite their being among the top ten most valuable brands in the world, you likely don't know their slogans.[2] Keep in mind that these brands spend billions—*billions*—on marketing.

The lesson is simple: Slogans aren't magic. In most cases, consumers don't pay much attention to them. Brands that focus too much on slogans end up neglecting the truly important aspects of their efforts.

Take McDonald's. Its longtime slogan, "I'm lovin' it," tends to perform well in surveys, primarily because it was launched all the way back in 2003.[3] But its previous tagline, "We love to see you smile," fell flat. The problem wasn't that it didn't roll off the tongue well enough or that it was contrary to the Golden Arches' brand idea. The fast-food giant stumbled because its slogan's underlying message wasn't being translated down to the store level. McDonald's simply wasn't making people smile like it used to.

Rule No. 1 in slogan making is to not advertise your aspirations. Saying "We love to see you smile" or "Quality is Job One" challenges cynical consumers to prove you wrong, which they're all too happy to do. The last thing you want to do is put forth an empty slogan that doesn't deliver.

Rule No. 2 is to give your slogan time to develop. State Farm's "Like a good neighbor" and Allstate's "The Good Hands People" have lasted for generations. Both have had time to seep into the consciousness of the marketplace. Brands that change their slogans too often never give them a chance to take root. You have to be patient.

Rule No. 3? Consider not using a slogan at all. After all, people may have a hard time remembering taglines for Starbucks, Mercedes, or Aveda, but they still pay a premium for the brands. While a slogan can be an excellent ribbon to wrap around your brand identity, it's not the sum and substance of it. Slogans, and the ad campaigns that deliver them, come and go. But great brands are timeless.

The key is to focus less on a slogan and more on your brand idea. Make sure it's relevant to your core target and consistently executed in the marketplace. If a good turn of phrase happens to capture the essence of that identity, use it. But don't expect a catchy expression to make up for a lack of value. The best motto in the world won't stop your customers from wondering "Where's the beef?"

A slogan is the ribbon around the package, not the prize inside.

33
TESTING MAY FAIL

IT MAY SEEM ODD THAT ANYBODY WOULD HAVE A PROBLEM WITH pretesting an ad or branding campaign. It's hard to argue with the potentially money-saving (and mistake-preventing) insights research can provide. And in theory, pretesting makes total sense. The problem is that the science of advertising pretesting just isn't there yet.

I came across a report in one of my trade publications that highlighted well the uncertainties of ad testing.[1] It cited Volkswagen's now-iconic "Da, Da, Da" commercial, which apparently some on VW's management team didn't want produced. But it was, and history proved them wrong.

The article went on to say that a handful of Volkswagen commercials were then evaluated using GM's custom-designed pretesting system. According to the report, the successful VW commercials flunked under GM's process. Now, which brand's advertising is more effective? Year after year, Volkswagen captures handfuls of international advertising awards, and its market share has more than doubled since 2007.[2] GM can't exactly claim the same results.

Why can't pretesting always predict what will happen in the real world? There are many reasons, but I believe they all essentially boil down to this: It is impossible to replicate in a research situation how somebody will respond to an ad on a Sunday afternoon, sitting in an easy chair munching on nachos and watching the game.

When people are invited to participate in market research, whether it's an online survey, a focus group, or even an in-home study, the circumstances themselves will change subjects' behavior. They know they're being watched, and they may even believe that their job is to be critical.

Think about how a focus group works: People are invited in, fed a meal, and paid an incentive to offer insights and opinions that the sponsoring brand can use. The pressure is on to contribute something of value. For people to admit that they simply like an ad or to confess that it might influence them to buy something is rare. Instead, participants tend to understate how much they are affected by advertising and be overly critical of the ads themselves.

But the desire to contribute isn't the only problem. Even if respondents in focus groups wanted to give an honest opinion, they may not be able to. People just aren't able to articulate or even understand all the ways branding affects them.

> **There's no better research laboratory than the real world.**

Marsha Lindsay, a member of the executive committee of the American Association of Advertising Agencies, explains the problem this way: "Copy testing and other research based on explicit learning cannot accurately predict ads' success because consumers can't tell us 'the truth' about how ads affect them. That learning often lies buried in their subconscious."[3] Stanford psychologist Robert Zajonc suggests that the more people see the same thing, the more they like it—but that people often don't initially like rare or unfamiliar things.[4] Commenting on Zajonc's research, Bruce Tait of Fallon Brand Consulting says:

> If brands are to succeed, they need to be based on differentiated, unfamiliar brand strategies. Unfortunately, these are the exact same ideas that people initially dislike.
>
> That's why quantitative testing of alternative positioning ideas will likely systematically kill the more original ideas, and people will prefer the ones that are closest to what they already know. The marketer using this type of test will unwittingly select the strategy that is less differentiated and eventually fail in the marketplace.[5]

By contrast, consider what the people behind some of the marketplace's most successful—and beloved—advertising have to say. Scott Bedbury, the former worldwide advertising director at Nike, says, "We never pretested anything we did at Nike, none of the ads. [Dan] Wieden [the founder of Wieden & Kennedy, Nike's advertising agency] and I had an agreement that as long as our hearts beat, we would never pretest a word of copy. It makes you dull. It makes you predictable. It makes you safe."[6]

Indeed, being creative is by definition being different, and being different is risky. Goodby, Silverstein & Partners is one of America's most accomplished advertising agencies. John Steel, the agency's first director of strategic planning, summarizes his experience with pretesting this way:

> I recently put together a reel of advertising . . . including "Got milk?" Polaroid, Isuzu Rodeo, Norwegian Cruise Line, and others. . . . All were extremely effective in building the client's business. Yet all could easily have died in creative development research had consumer comments been listened to literally, creatives not been allowed to express their differing opinions, and the client in each case not had the courage to say, "I hear what they are saying, but I will not change my mind about running this advertising as a result."[7]

Because of the limitations of the science of pretesting, the only truly reliable form of research is the real world—in a test market situation, for example, or by using tracking studies. Even these have their limits, and the results must be interpreted carefully. But at least these methods are based on what happens in real time, in the real world—not on what respondents think might happen.

Use research to explore, not to decide. Studies and surveys can tell us a lot of things, but they can't predict the future. As Tait puts it, "Statistical reliability is not the same thing as the truth."[8]

34
GIVING GETS

I'LL NEVER FORGET THE FIRST TIME I STAYED AT A RITZ-CARLTON hotel. (No, it doesn't happen that often.) When I pulled up into the stunning circular drive, my door was gently opened by a smiling valet who didn't let me worry for a moment about where I was to go or who would handle my bags. Upon entering the hotel, I was greeted by name by a charming young man who offered me a complimentary glass of champagne. The front desk clerk was impeccably polite as she checked me in, told me about the hotel, and made sure my bags met me at my room. The experience pretty much continued that way for the length of my stay. Everybody was so . . . considerate.

I'm not naive. I know that the way I was being treated, while sincere, was made possible by the fact that the organization that put me up at the Ritz was paying a pretty penny to do so. But I still felt special. Ritz-Carlton's brand idea of "ladies and gentlemen serving ladies and gentlemen" was unfolding before my eyes, and I appreciated it. It was a gift that I gladly accepted.

"Brand as gift" is an apt metaphor. A fair paraphrase of the textbook definition of marketing is that it's about finding out what people want and giving it to them. There are numerous parallels between the art of branding and the art of gift giving.

First, gift giving should be about what the recipient will like, not what you like. Have you ever picked out a present you really wanted someone to have, only to be disappointed that they didn't welcome it as you had intended? That might be because you gave them what *you* wanted to give them, not what they wanted to receive. Similarly, the best branding is developed with the audience's needs in mind. It not only wins their attention, it wins their affection as well. Do this repeatedly and you'll be someone they want to hang around. Do it often enough and you'll get a reputation as a great gift giver, which will get you invited to a lot of parties.

Second, you can't give to everyone, so begin with those you love. While it would be nice to give something to everybody, it's simply unaffordable. As we saw in chapter 1, you can't make the whole world your target audience; if you try, you won't make an effective impact on anybody. Just as your gift giving is "targeted" toward the people you value most, your branding efforts should be targeted toward the customers and prospects you value most. It's the only way to make a lasting impression.

> **The best way to get something is to give something first.**

Third, gratitude is the fruit of thoughtfulness, in branding as in gift giving. Currency is nice, but it's not very thoughtful. It's easy to slip someone a gift card, discount, or loyalty program points. It's also lazy. The problem with something that can be counted is that its value is transparent: It is what it is, nothing more. You don't get credit for being thoughtful and understanding when you give currency—because you haven't been. Perhaps the worst thing about giving away currency is that it establishes a benchmark; if you give less of it next time, your gift will be greeted with diminished enthusiasm. Branding is a tool to enhance relationships, not cheapen them. Don't use points, discounts, or rebates to bribe people.

Fourth, appliances aren't gifts. One day when my wife and I were strolling the aisles of our local home improvement store, she remarked that perhaps it's time we got a Shop-Vac. I joked that I would put it on her Christmas list. She didn't laugh.

When you're giving a gift, you're not conducting a transaction. (Here's your present, honey. Go vacuum the car.) You're investing in a relationship that will be mutually rewarding over time. Similarly, if your branding is always accompanied by an expectation, it may not be received in the manner you would like.

Finally, don't forget that wrapping makes a difference. A box swathed in beautiful paper, lovingly tied with a colorful bow, is a lot more enticing than a rumpled paper sack. Gifts' "production values" not only make them more visually appealing, they communicate to recipients that you value them enough to spend the time and money to make your presentation special. The less attractive the package, the more likely the intended recipient will be to leave it unnoticed and unopened.

Branding, like life, really isn't all that complicated. If you give joyfully, consistently, and thoughtfully, your giving will not only bless others. It will bless you too. Give to give, not merely to get, and you're likely to find that you benefit most of all.

35
LESS IS OFTEN MORE

WHEN MEGA-TV HIT *LOST* AIRED ITS FINAL EPISODE, THE COM-
mercials sold for nearly a million dollars a spot. Of specific note were
the Target ads, which took unique advantage of the event by having
fun with historical *LOST* plotlines, tying them to computer keyboards,
barbecue sauce, and smoke alarms, among other things. The products
themselves didn't matter, as they were just pegs for punch lines of what
amounted to inside jokes.

Those jokes are what made Target's strategy so smart. By tying its
spots to *LOST*'s imagery and icons, not only did the commercials command viewers' attention, they effectively said, "Hey, Target's a *LOST* fan
too. We get it." It was as if Target had been sitting down in front of the
tube right alongside every *LOST* viewer for six years.

People do business with brands they trust, and sharing common experiences builds trust. During the *LOST* season finale, Target reinforced
its friendship with millions of customers who are fanatical fans of the
show. Whether it sold more barbecue sauce or smoke alarms the next
day wasn't the point. Branding is about building awareness, preference,
and bonds of affection, and Target used its multimillion-dollar *LOST*
buy to do just that.

Contrast that with a radio commercial I heard from a national
health insurance company. I tuned in long enough to catch an announcer
drone on about features and benefits, copayments and deductibles. Then
I tuned out. I'm sure it was very interesting to the marketing people at
the insurance company, just not to me—or any of the thousands of other
listeners the business was trying to reach.

I've heard marketers justify cramming ads full of information by citing the high price of media and saying, "We need to get our money's worth." Yes, media costs a lot, and every advertiser needs its ads to work as hard as possible. But just as getting your money's worth at a buffet doesn't mean stuffing your face, reaping return on investment from branding doesn't require inundating your audience with facts, claims, and comparisons. That approach will just give them a headache.

Don't confuse branding with journalism. Journalism's mission is to inform the audience by presenting all the relevant facts about a given topic. It works because people seek out the news intentionally—they want to read and hear and see what's going on.

> **Your advertising isn't about your brand. It's an extension of it.**

But advertising is different. People tolerate advertising because they know it helps pay for media they enjoy, but they're also quite adept at tuning it out. For that reason, advertising needs to come across more like theater.

Over the years, an unspoken social contract has developed. Consumers effectively tell brands, "Entertain me, and I will give you my attention. Respect my intelligence, and I'll give you my interest. Do neither, and I'll give you neither." Those brands that respect the contract enjoy success. Those who don't end up complaining advertising doesn't work.

Years ago, John Hancock Insurance introduced the "Real Life, Real Answers" campaign. The commercials seemed less like ads and more like mini-movies, dramatizing two brothers talking or a middle-age man choking up as he reads his fiftieth-birthday card. The campaign didn't attempt to hammer home a heavy sales message and didn't even say anything concrete about John Hancock. It simply drew the viewers in and let them come to their own conclusions. Oh, and it generated a 17 percent sales increase.[1]

Apple's "1984" commercial aired only twice—and is widely credited with starting the Super Bowl advertising craze. (The second airing was on a local station in the middle of the night, just to qualify for 1983 advertising awards.) What most people don't remember is that the commercial featured no real dialogue other than a simple concluding statement: "On January 24, Apple Computer will introduce Macintosh. And you'll see why 1984 won't be like '1984.'"

Apple set out to hold the interest of the audience through two minutes of the most expensive TV time available, using not facts, claims, or comparisons but a storyline. It didn't try to explain why 1984 would differ from *1984* (the book) but instead trusted the audience to complete the picture. The audience did, and the ad, like the product, went down in history.

Sure, "1984" required a big-budget production, but this kind of approach doesn't necessarily call for massive funding. You can achieve it via a simple image on a billboard or dialogue in a radio spot. What it does require is empathy for the audience and the knowledge that the key to success is drawing people in and letting them complete the picture for themselves. It requires a little restraint on behalf of the brand. That's when powerful impressions are made.

Most ads try to spoon-feed people. But nobody past the age of six months wants spoon-feeding. Take a different approach. Draw people in. Tell a story. Encourage them to engage in it, and reward them when they do. If you do it right, they'll want to see your ads again and again. And then you'll really start getting your money's worth.

36
GAPS ARE GOOD

REMEMBER THOSE CONNECT-THE-DOTS ILLUSTRATIONS THAT DE-lighted us as children? Simply by taking a pencil and drawing a line from one dot to the next, then to another and another, we played a part in bringing a picture into being. As we did, we experienced the joy that comes with creation. Even though the dots were laid out by somebody else, the act of connecting them made the picture our own, and some-times our moms even pinned the results to the refrigerator door.

That's not only the approach Apple took with "1984," it's what put Monster.com on the map via a much-talked-about 60 seconds of air-time. The commercial showed cute kids proudly declaring that when they grow up they want to become not what you'd expect—doctors, as-tronauts, professional athletes—but instead "claw my way up to middle management," "be replaced on a whim," and "be paid less for doing the same job," among other career nightmares. The spot ended with a simple question: "What do you want to be?" It was a creative connect-the-dots game that, with just a little bit of thought, led viewers to view Monster. com as the antidote to a dead-end job.

As marketers, it's our job to think ahead and set the dots in such a way as to enable our audience to complete the picture. Another way of thinking of it is that we make spark plugs, and it's our job to leave a gap just wide enough to generate the spark of an idea or realization in our audience.

Here's how the real-life spark plug experts at the Green Spark Plug Co. in Cheshire, England, describe what the goal should be: "The gap adjustment can be fairly critical. A narrow gap may give too small and weak a spark to effectively ignite the fuel–air mixture, while a gap that is too wide might prevent a spark from firing at all."[1]

When GM released its Cadillac CTS Sport Wagon, it calibrated the gap for a sophisticated audience in a full-page newspaper ad. The ad pictured a beauty shot of the car under the simple headline "Sorry About the Applecart." It took me a minute (just one, mind you) to realize what the ad was trying to say, but when I did, I was pleased because I was in on the joke. Cadillac buyers aren't dummies, and by reflecting an understanding of that in its advertising, the brand made itself look smart.

It can be tough to resist the temptation to bridge the gap for our customers, but the most effective branding merely starts a thought, allowing the audience to finish it. By drawing their own conclusions, they're more likely to be convinced, and the result is more likely to stick because they invited the thought into their minds rather than raising their defenses to shut it out.

> **People are more likely to remember a picture they helped complete.**

Ernest Hemingway was once challenged to tell an entire story in a mere six words. His solution—"For sale: baby shoes, never used"—is a sublime example of the gap principle. Hemingway left it to the reader to bridge the gap—the tragedy, the sadness, the grief—in his short but compelling tale. No two readers imagine what happened in exactly the same way, making each story, by definition, personally theirs. Since they own it, they're likely never to forget it—and they just might share it with someone else.

Minding this gap is not an easy thing, and as creators of brand messaging, we have our work cut out for us. But it's much more fun (and effective) to spend our energy influencing people toward the right conclusions rather than presuming we can tell them what to think. Hemingway also said: "If a writer knows enough about what he is writing about, he may omit things that he knows. The dignity of movement of an iceberg is due to only one-ninth of it being above water."[2]

Nobody wants to be told what to think. When we allow the audience to connect the dots, to complete the story, to bridge the gap, they own the outcome. It's true in children's art, it's true in literature, and it's true in branding. All we need to make it work is imagination, respect for our audience, and the confidence that when they complete the thought, it will spark a reaction.

37

NOT ALL BELLS ARE EQUAL

ONE DAY AS I WAS LEAVING WORK, I NOTICED THE SOUND OF bells coming from the parochial school down the road. I paused for a moment and took in the chimes as they marked the top of the hour. The sound made me smile and somehow put the cares of the day in perspective. Most people probably feel the same way about the comforting sound of church bells. They usually herald something good.

Unfortunately, in our fast-paced culture, the bells we hear are more often annoying than pleasant. I live in a neighborhood filled with home alarm systems. Many of my neighbors set their alarms each night and forget all about them when they get up for a midnight snack or a trip to the bathroom. It seems as if at least once a week the neighborhood is jolted awake by an alarm going off in the middle of the night. The seconds turn into minutes (which seem like hours) as the offending homeowner stumbles through the dark to find the keypad and disarm the system. And heaven forbid he's out of town when a false alarm goes off.

Both church bells and alarm bells cause a ringing in the ear. Yet the way people react to each is different; one evokes positive thoughts and warm feelings, the other annoyance. It's a good metaphor for branding.

Consider tone. Church bells are meant to be musical. They're designed to please the ear as they celebrate weddings, holidays, or simply mark the passing hours. Their role is to bring pleasure and harmony to a community. MasterCard has mastered the church-bell approach to advertising with its long-running "Priceless" campaign, tapping into universal emotions and associating its credit cards with "everything that matters." MasterCard ads aren't interruptive, they're inviting.

By contrast, alarm bells are meant to steal attention—to command interest, assert an urgent need, and force someone to do something. Do you have casinos and car dealers that advertise in your town? I'm willing to bet they're a good example of alarm-bell branding.

Brands that believe in the alarm-bell approach want their advertising to be intrusive and attention getting, so they do everything they can to get the audience's notice. They believe that by turning up the volume and making the right pitch, people will be bound to do business with them. But none of us likes to be told what to do, especially if, in the telling, the advertiser passes the red line on our annoyance meter.

> **A brand, like a bell, is defined by its tone.**

Now consider the source. Church bells come from a place of tradition, history, and community. They represent service and humility. They're like the old AT&T, encouraging us to "reach out and touch someone." But alarm bells come from a machine—an electronic box, an impersonal mishmash of wires and transistors with no knowledge of, or concern for, those who may be annoyed by them. This is more like today's telecommunications advertising, offering the deal of the month on mobile minutes and text messaging.

If you think of branding as purely mechanistic, don't expect to create a lot of goodwill. If "sales" is all it's about, then sales are all you'll get. You might think that's fine until you get locked into a death spiral of commoditization where the prize goes to the lowest bidder. Demonstrate respect, intelligence, or thoughtfulness, however, and you'll build equity that can be counted on.

What about the message? If there ever were a real emergency in my neighborhood, I think most people would ignore it, presuming it was just another false alarm. That's the problem with alarm-bell branding. We've simply seen (or heard) too much of it. Like the boy who cried wolf, the advertiser who cries "Sale!" has disappointed us too many times.

That simply reinforces the wisdom of the church-bell approach: People are so conditioned to dismiss self-serving branding approaches that they're likely to be pleasantly surprised by—and pay attention to—advertising that respects their emotions and intelligence. That's how a campaign such as MasterCard's can last for so long and expand to dozens of languages in more than 100 countries.[1] Its appeal is universal.

Finally, there's timing. Both church bells and alarm bells offer valuable information. But alarm bells, by their very nature, tend to go off when you least want to hear them. No one ever wants to be exposed to alarm-bell advertising. It may capture people's attention, but it will never gain their affection. When was the last time you heard an alarm go off anywhere and it spurred you to think happy thoughts?

Church bells are different. When church bells ring, something good has happened. School is out. Someone just got married. The war has ended. Church bells bring good news at a good time. Church bell advertising is something people welcome. Church bells attract. Alarm bells repel.

Do you want your branding to make people pause, smile, and think good thoughts? Or would you prefer it to jolt them out of bed and into action? Both approaches can gain attention, but only one leaves people feeling better. If you want to build long-term equity among your customers and prospects, take a church-bell approach.

38
PROMISES ARE PROBLEMATIC

OK, I'LL ADMIT IT. AS A (GRACEFULLY) AGING MAN, I NO LONGER fit the sweet spot of McDonald's core customer profile. No matter how much I remain tempted by the taste of its burgers, I just can't pack them in with the reckless abandon I did 20 years (and 20 pounds) ago. I now tend to opt for healthier food in a more comfortable environment that better fits my, ahem, maturing tastes.

Back when I was a gut-stuffing young man, however, I didn't drool over Quarter Pounders alone. Just about any fast-food place would do, as long as the burgers were big, the fries were salty, and the drive-through was fast. Yet there's one thing that McDonald's—and only McDonald's—could give me. Oddly enough, it's something the brand never overtly promised. It wasn't even presented in a form with which I could argue.

I didn't realize what McDonald's had done until I became a father and my son came of age to play Little League. It was only after he first tested his mettle on the field that the thought struck me: Where else were he and his dad going to regale his accomplishments and plot his Major League career but under the Golden Arches? Images of fathers and sons sharing a postgame moment over a big red box of fries have been playing over and over in my head ever since McDonald's first seeded them there when I was a boy myself. Taking your son to McDonald's after a game—well, that's what a dad is supposed to do.

Half a century ago, McDonald's was one of the first advertisers to understand that brand building isn't about making claims, promises, and offers. It's about making emotional connections—connections that associate positive feelings, not disputable data—with a product or service. In fact, as our consumer culture has grown ever more sophisticated, it has become more dangerous than ever to aim ads at the left brain.

For one, claims can be challenged. If McDonald's were to claim that its fries were somehow "the best"—even if it had indisputable market research proving that three out of five people believed just that—any individual customer might personally favor the fries at Wendy's or Burger King. Customers might even convince themselves that's the case so they don't feel like mindless sheep. Make a claim and you dare people to challenge it.

> **Be careful that your promise isn't seen as a dare.**

Promises can be problematic as well. McDonald's has probably served the perfect French fry somewhere to someone, and perhaps even more than once. The fries are pretty darn consistent, I'll give McDonald's that. But there has inevitably been a time when the grease was too hot, the warming lamp burned out, or the 17-year-old manning the fry station was too tired from a late night that the product just didn't deliver. Promise perfection, and you'll dare customers to catch you in an inevitable imperfect moment.

That's not to say that a brand should never tout its virtues or provide relevant, compelling information to prospective customers. There is a time and place to do that in the context of a broad-based, integrated marketing program. But science is bearing out why the right-brain approach that McDonald's, Coca-Cola, Budweiser, and so many other master marketers have adopted works.

Research by Jonah Berger of the Wharton School at the University of Pennsylvania has shown that emotional arousal makes people much more likely to share information, accounting for why the most popular Internet videos are about cute, touching, or hilarious moments, not interesting and unusual factoids.[1]

It's not a stretch to apply Berger's research to branding. When people's emotions are engaged, their interest goes up and their defenses go down—exactly the right environment in which to make a compelling connection.

McDonald's was one of the first advertisers to really understand this. Decades ago, when its competitors were boasting about the size of their burgers or the thickness of their shakes, McDonald's was busy crafting emotional portraits of families enjoying moments of togetherness around a fast-food lunch. Consumers could easily accept or reject the rational claims being made by competitors, but the poignant appeals pioneered by McDonald's changed the playing field. Instead of a binary true-or-false equation, these emotional slices of life were hard to argue against and easy to embrace.

Sure, the commercials I've just described seem quaint today, and the tactics of emotional branding have evolved over time as consumers have become more sophisticated, but the underlying principle remains true.

It can be difficult to refrain from boasting about the merits of your products or services. But if you want people to feel good about what you have to offer, focus on making them feel good. They're smart enough to connect the dots, and when they do, your brand will get the credit.

39
CREATIVITY SELLS

HAVE YOU MET THE MOST INTERESTING MAN IN THE WORLD? "HE lives vicariously through himself. He once had an awkward moment, just to see how it feels. His shirts never wrinkle. Cuba imports cigars from him. In museums, he is allowed to touch the art. And he has won the lifetime achievement award, twice."[1]

I'm speaking, of course, of the famous Dos Equis pitchman who became a cultural icon and propelled the Mexican beer to a rate of growth five times greater than the average of the top ten imported beers.[2] The branding effort captivated beer drinkers and made a huge difference in the bottom line of Heineken, USA, Dos Equis's importer.

Creativity is at the heart of every branding campaign. But critics of advertising often put forth the challenge that creativity is frivolous, since many examples of so-called creativity haven't sold a thing. While these ads may win awards, they're not effective in the marketplace, so they say. And in some cases they're correct.

But creativity itself gets a bum rap. The question of whether creativity sells is never asked of movies, art, or music. Of course it sells; just ask Dos Equis—or Disney, Pixar, or the Beatles. Creativity, in the proper context, always outperforms the absence of it.

It's particularly critical for smaller brands to understand this. Because of their size, they must use every element of creativity at their disposal to overcome the budget advantage of larger competitors. One of the reasons small brands struggle with this issue is because they are asking the wrong questions: Creativity or effectiveness? Sizzle or sales? Image or product? These are false choices. Creativity and effectiveness are really two sides of the same coin.

The key to making branding effective is to create trust—trust that the product or service will meet a need, trust that it will be of value, and trust that there will be no surprises. Trust is the common factor that every great brand delivers, whether it's beer, pizza, pet stores, or dish soap. And what's a proven way to create trust? You guessed it: creativity.

Salespeople intuitively understand this. Trust is based on familiarity, chemistry, and at least some level of affection. Every good salesperson is adept at building this kind of trust, knowing that the sale seldom comes down to objective criteria alone but involves some level of good feelings about the person delivering the message. Good salespeople never go about generating these positive feelings in exactly the same way. They approach each prospective client in a fashion tailored specifically for him or her. They use their creativity.

> **It doesn't matter how good your brand is if no one pays attention.**

Rarely, however, can a company personally call on all of its prospects. That's when branding must fulfill the role of building trust. In this respect, any business can learn a lot from Dos Equis.

In its ads, Dos Equis relates to the audience, respects their intelligence, and rewards them for paying attention with a chuckle. And in return, the audience votes with its pocketbook for the brand. Brands like Dos Equis understand that their advertising is less *about* them than it is an *extension* of them. If consumers like an ad, they will typically like the advertiser. Truly creative branding presents the virtues of a product or service in a likable context. It's that simple (and that difficult).

It's true that creativity outside of a strategic context won't do anybody any good other than win awards. At the same time, however, brands must avoid the fallacy of rationality that reduces buying decisions to mechanical trade-offs between costs and benefits. As we've seen, people just don't work that way.

The best advertising, like a beautiful painting or well-crafted movie, should be stirring, moving, thought provoking, even uplifting. Must it be strategic? Of course—but even the best strategy won't compensate for a lack of imagination.

40
PARTNERSHIPS PAY

GOT A SPARE FIFTY THOUSAND BUCKS LYING AROUND? IT'S AL-most enough to get you a new pickup truck. Ford's F-150 Harley-Davidson Super Crew is not only a powerful work truck loaded with options, it's cobranded with one of the most iconic names in transpor-tation. That's why Ford can charge a premium and why both it and its partner, Harley-Davidson, reap enhanced equity from the relationship.

Cobranding is nothing new. Visit a grocery store and you'll see doz-ens of examples, from the ice cream aisle (Breyer's and Hershey), to the snack aisle (Lay's and KC Masterpiece), to the cereal aisle (Kellogg's and Healthy Choice), to the dessert aisle (Cinnabon and Mrs. Smith's). You can also find cobranding examples in the hospitality industry (Bul-gari and Ritz-Carlton), the footwear business (Disney and Crocs), the franchising world (Tim Hortons and Cold Stone), the airline industry (Southwest and SeaWorld), and even product catalogs stuffed into air-plane seat pockets ("Order your Braun Oral-B Plaque Remover today").

There are a number of reasons companies embark on cobranding programs. To begin with, they're a convenient way of introducing one company's products and services to the loyalists of another. Perhaps the best example of this is the now-legendary "Intel Inside" campaign, which launched a brand that few consumers had ever heard of into the stratosphere by piggybacking on the equity of big computer makers, such as IBM and HP. Within a year of the program's launch, Intel was cobranding with some 300 computer manufacturers.

Cobranding also enables one brand to benefit from the halo of af-fection that belongs to another. That was the rationale behind Nike's original 1984 alliance with Michael Jordan, and the effort has done wonders for both.

Another benefit of cobranding is cost savings. That's one reason you increasingly see fast-food restaurants like Pizza Hut and Taco Bell sharing the same building—and sometimes the same counter, menu boards, and staff. But cobranding is not just for giant national or international brands. While a small brand may have difficulty linking up with Nike or Procter & Gamble, many businesses can avail themselves of an increasing number of off-the-shelf cobranding opportunities.

Programs have been developed by credit card companies such as Visa and MasterCard, retailers including Starbucks and Barnes & Noble, and even shipping companies—the U.S. Postal Service offers a service by which any company can add its company logo to its Priority Mail packaging.

> **Brands that help each other help themselves.**

Beyond these, there are bound to be dozens of custom cobranding partners for just about any type of business, whether you serve a local geographical area or a national vertical market. The key is to think creatively about products or services that complement yours in some way and that will enhance the appeal or credibility of your offering.

For example, a restaurant could cobrand with a local packaged-foods maker to create a new menu item, an accounting firm could cobrand with an information technology provider to create a new consulting offering, or a physician might cobrand with a hospital on a new service line. A good place to start generating ideas is by thinking about other types of companies that do a good job serving your target market. You might even ask your customers to identify other companies with which they do business and see if you come across any patterns.

Be careful, however—cobranding is not without its risks. It can have a dilutive effect, since it spreads the credit for a positive experience across two brands where normally there's only one. And if the experience isn't positive—even if it's the other brand's fault—it may reflect negatively on you. (Not to pick on the Postal Service, but if your company's name is on the side of a Priority Mail package, how does it reflect on you if it arrives late or damaged?) Further, when you cobrand, you are to some extent relying on another brand's equity. That can, in some cases, make your brand look weak or secondary.

It's important, therefore, to carefully consider your own cobranding principles before you enter the fray. Develop guidelines that are right for your business that will enable you to objectively assess opportunities that arise. Many large corporations have set out formal guidelines for this purpose—AT&T even put a Co-Branding Decision Tool on its intranet to help guide managers through a variety of decision factors related to cobranding opportunities.

While many brands share similar characteristics, no two are exactly alike. Cobranding ice cream and root beer is a natural; cobranding sports cars and computers, less so (though that didn't prevent Ferrari from linking up with Acer). Ecco Shoes cobranding with the World Wide Fund for Nature makes intuitive sense; Chanel and Hello Kitty is a bit more of a head-scratcher. Look for brand fit not only from the perspective of attributes and benefits but also with respect to core values and corporate philosophies.

Cobranding is an often-overlooked strategy by which the whole can truly be greater than the sum of the parts. While it should be used sparingly and judiciously, it could generate a new level of interest and excitement around your products and services.

41

BORING IS CRIMINAL

IKEA, THE SWEDEN-BASED GLOBAL FURNITURE CHAIN, IS KNOWN almost as much for its creative branding as it is for its huge selection and giant, maze-like showrooms. Whether it's an iconic television commercial starring a discarded lamp, subway displays that make a tunnel look like home, chalk art that makes two-dimensional sidewalks appear as three-dimensional living spaces, or a campaign that produces a new commercial every day for a year, IKEA knows how to captivate its customers and prospects.

Contrast that with an AdweekMedia poll that posed this question: "Of the ads you see in a typical day, how many engage your attention?" A remarkable two-thirds of respondents said "a small minority of them." Another quarter answered "none of them." Together, that's more than nine out of ten people.[1]

Ouch. While polls like these have their limitations (we often can't—or won't—tell the truth about our own purchase behavior), I suspect few us would doubt the overall conclusion that a lot of advertising doesn't work very well. Your own ads may even fall into that category. A lot of advertising is, frankly, boring.

Why do people watch TV, listen to the radio, read the newspaper, or go online? Three reasons: information, entertainment, and engagement. Ads that fail to offer at least two of these three benefits flop. Just as nobody reads every story in the newspaper, nobody pays attention to every ad.

As the poll demonstrates, most people don't engage with most ads. And even when they do, for how long do they pay attention? Thirty seconds? Ten? Five? The best an ad can do is communicate one single, compelling idea, and in the age of the Internet—when people know they can go online to get all the additional information they need—it's crazy to ask an ad to do more than that.

Just because you have a lot to say doesn't mean your audience will sit still and pay attention. Instead, engage your prospects with something that is interesting or entertaining, and they'll give you their valuable time and attention.

To do so, you need to be able to consistently step out of your own shoes and into the shoes of your customers. That's not always easy. My firm worked with a franchise company whose target audience is a unique type of white-collar woman, while most of its franchisees are blue-collar men. We learned the hard way that developing a brand message that rings the bell of its female target audience caused members of the franchisee community to scratch their heads. They just didn't get it.

> **You have to engage your customers before they'll engage with your brand.**

It also means that you'll have to move at their pace, not yours. You can't rush bread out of the oven and you can't hurry a seedling out of the ground. All you can do is prepare the ingredients properly, tend the garden with care, and wait for the loaf to rise or sprouts to appear. If you expect too much too soon (especially on a limited budget), you're sure to be disappointed.

Think about your own consumer behavior—how many times do you need to be exposed to a marketing message before you take action? Depending on your prospects' level of interest in the category and frequency of purchase, it could take weeks, months, or even years for your message to sink in. I've never owned a Mercedes, but someday I might, and if I do, it will be the result of years of equity building Mercedes-Benz has invested in me.

There are, of course, many more reasons why advertising under-performs, from poor media placement, to bad strategy, to competitive countermoves. But the reason a lot of advertising fails to break through is that it's simply uninteresting to those to whom it's ostensibly targeted. Being different isn't in and of itself a guarantee of success, but as IKEA repeatedly demonstrates, what you do is a lot more likely to get noticed if it hasn't been done before.

42

HUMOR HELPS

YOU WOULDN'T THINK AN AD FOR LAUNDRY DETERGENT COULD be engaging. And for decades, apparently neither did the makers of laundry detergent. The category's advertising was marked by predictable formulations: After a setup of a frustrated wife wringing her hands about "ring around the collar" or a perfect mom preening about her "whitest whites," a pitchman underscores the detergent's promise while clean clothes dance in a dryer or wave in a warm summer breeze. Yawn.

Then came Procter & Gamble with its Tide to Go stain remover pen, a handy embarrassment-avoidance device that anyone could carry along in a purse or briefcase. Tide and its agency, Saatchi & Saatchi, came up with an innovative television commercial that would break category conventions by dramatizing the problem solved by Tide to Go in a way that just about anyone could relate to: the dreaded job interview.

The scene is simple, and it happens thousands of times a day in offices everywhere: An accomplished-looking older gentleman leans across his desk toward the earnest (and nervous) interviewee and says, "Tell me about yourself." In the most confident way he can, the young applicant begins reciting his rehearsed qualifications. There's just one problem: As the young man speaks, the sound of his words is drowned out by a stain on his shirt that rudely shouts over everything he says. The camera cuts back to the interviewer, who's is doing his best to concentrate as his eyes dart back and forth between the young man's face and the stain on his shirt. The interchange, needless to say, does not go well.

The commercial is a great example of the connect-the-dots principle. Rather than being told what is happening, viewers have to pick it up along the way, and by the time most of us are in on the joke, a well-timed signature line appears on-screen: "Silence the stain, instantly." The commercial immediately made Tide to Go the talk of the water cooler set, and within ten days of its first airing during the Super Bowl, it generated more than 15,000 hours of engagement at a Web site to which it was tied.[1] It was effective on a number of levels, not the least of which was it is just plain funny.

Humor can work so well in branding it's a wonder more brands don't pursue it. Perhaps it's because it's easily thought of as frivolous. But before you dismiss wit as incompatible with your marketing objectives, consider how (and why) it works.

> **A humorous brand is a confident brand, and a confident brand is attractive.**

Humor is powerful in part because it connects people. The only way someone can make you laugh is if they understand something about you, sharing in common your sense of humor if nothing else. A laugh represents a nice little moment of connection, whether shared between two people or between a brand and its prospective customers.

Humor is also effective because it's enjoyable. When we hear a great joke or see something funny we're inclined to want more, so we'll watch funny videos again and again and do our best to remember the great joke we heard at the office. When people enjoy an experience, they want to replicate it. Even if it's an ad.

Another branding benefit is that humor is social by nature; people are instinctively inclined to spread that which they find funny. Not all of us are good at telling jokes, but when we hear a good one, we'll do our best to share it with others. It's no secret (and should be no surprise) that the most viral of videos on the Web tend to be those that do the best jobs tickling people's funny bones. Evian's "Roller Babies" and "Baby & Me" YouTube videos became online sensations seen by tens of millions of people around the world simply because they're so lighthearted and enjoyable to watch.[2]

Another benefit of humor is that it's a force multiplier when it comes to limited marketing budgets. Evian doesn't have to pay a dime to distribute its fun (and funny) content; people like you and me are happy to do all the work.

When the lights went out unexpectedly on Super Bowl XLVII, Oreo smelled a similar opportunity and sent a tweet featuring a shadowy image of its signature cookie accompanied by the simple headline "You can still dunk in the dark." The brand quickly became a trending topic on Twitter, and as of noon the following day, the message had been retweeted more than 15,000 times.[3] Audi also got into the power outage act by posting a tweet that tweaked rival Mercedes-Benz, sponsor of the dimly lit Superdome where the game was held. Both auto brands got a great deal of attention at virtually no cost.

Humor has its downsides, of course. There's nothing worse than telling a joke that falls flat, and it's easy to get distracted by something that may be funny but isn't strategic; witness Kmart's "Ship My Pants" and "Big Gas Savings" ads, which used sophomoric humor that not only obscured the message but risked offending its core customers. Like any form of creativity, if it's not strategic it's not smart, regardless of how funny it may be.

You may not have the budget to hire expensive directors or produce high-end TV commercials. But as Oreo and Audi demonstrated, any brand with an understanding of its audience and a little imagination can use humor effectively, in any form of media. Being winsome and engaging will always go a long way.

43

MANNERS MATTER

SOME PEOPLE LOVE COCKTAIL PARTIES. I CALL THEM "NETWORK-ers." You know the type. They waltz into the room, scan it to see who's there, and then begin working their way from person to person trying to distribute business cards and gather leads. Networkers are one of the reasons the rest of us dread cocktail parties. They make us feel like a bus stop.

Still, occasionally you'll meet someone at a cocktail party and find yourself engaged in a truly fascinating conversation. Sometimes someone so interesting will come along that time flies by and you hope neither a networker nor anybody else interrupts you. Sometimes those conversations evolve into business relationships and even friendships.

If you've been in business for any length of time, you've learned the cocktail-party etiquette that can lead to such a conversation: Focus on one person at a time. Make eye contact. Listen. Don't talk about yourself. Find what they're interested in and make that the topic of conversation. Most of all, don't be arrogant, boorish, or annoying. Following these simple rules will increase your odds of starting an interesting new relationship and decrease the chances you'll be perceived as someone to avoid.

By now it's probably no surprise to you that the same rules apply to branding.

Think about how you relate to most ads you see. You expect them to talk about themselves. You expect them to be loud. You expect them to tell you what they want you to hear rather than focusing on what's interesting to you. Most ads act like someone with bad manners at a cocktail party. They fail the cocktail-party test.

Of course, it's true that our expectations of a brand from an etiquette standpoint are somewhat lower than what we expect from human contact. We don't get offended by an annoying ad the same way we do by an overbearing networker. But the principles of human interaction hold true, and whether the annoyance is coming at us through the door or through the computer, it's something we want to avoid.

That's why many marketing programs underperform. Brands desperately want to have a relationship with their prospects, but the reverse doesn't always hold true. And the more a brand presses, the less likely it is that it will be well received. Just like at a cocktail party, brands have to win people over, not bowl them over.

What's the difference between the editorial features and the advertising in your favorite magazine? Simple. The editorial features are written with you, the reader, in mind. Their objective is to give you something, be it information, entertainment, or enlightenment, and that's why you pay good money for a subscription. Most of the ads, by contrast, are trying to sell you something. That's why you flip past them. If there's an ad or two in that magazine that focuses not on what it has to sell but on informing, entertaining, or otherwise pleasing you, it's much more likely to capture your interest and affection.

> **If you wouldn't do it at a cocktail party, don't do it in an ad.**

It's easy to get attention by shouting, jumping up and down, or acting inappropriately in some other way. But that's not the kind of attention you want. Meet your prospects where they are. Make eye contact with them, if you will, and demonstrate that you understand where they're coming from and what they're dealing with. Give them something of value—something interesting or funny or touching. As you make the moments they spend with your brand rewarding, don't be surprised if they want to spend more time with it.

44

BEHAVIOR ISN'T BELIEF

FROM THE EARLIEST DAYS OF COMMERCE, MERCHANTS HAVE RE-warded their most loyal customers with perks and points—from the baker's dozen to S&H Green Stamps. But in the modern era, customer loyalty programs became an industry all their own.

We owe that to American Airlines. Kick-started by the 1981 advent of American's AAdvantage program, total U.S. consumer membership in loyalty-marketing programs is now more than a billion strong. Financial services loyalty programs alone have more than 400 million members, airlines nearly 300 million, and even gambling operations have tied up more than 100 million customers in their frequent los . . . er . . . player programs.[1]

But are loyalty programs really all they're cracked up to be? McKinsey & Company reports that three-quarters of American households are enrolled in one or more and that the average household has registered for *18* of them. But the consultancy also reports that Americans are active in fewer than half of the loyalty programs of which they're members.[2]

And what of the programs in which people are active? Do these programs generate true loyalty or just behavior that looks like loyalty?

It's kind of frightening that, as consumers, we can be reduced to the contents of our wallets. I emptied my own and found that I carry seven cards from companies that track and reward my purchase behavior.

I feel genuine loyalty to three of those brands. Two others capture many of my transactions not because of any loyalty I feel but simply because of the benefits they give me. And two I use occasionally because I have a lot invested in them—given the way they've treated me over the years, they actually elicit mild contempt from me each time I do. Not exactly what the loyalty program is designed to generate.

And that's my point: If each of these brands judged my loyalty strictly by my behavior, they're going to the wrong idea about how I think. That's the problem with loyalty programs. "Loyalty," as it's defined in practice by loyalty marketing programs, is primarily a measure of behavior—share of wallet, if you will. But making decisions by share of wallet alone is a dangerous game.

Think about a brand's most active loyalty marketing program members. It's possible that many of them are the least genuinely "loyal" customers the brand has. As the data flows in and the brand increasingly tailors the program toward those whose behavior can be bought, it may be neglecting truly loyal customers who don't need to be bribed.

> **You can buy loyalty or you can build it. Don't take the shortcut.**

At least as important as share of wallet is share of heart, or what is commonly known as brand equity. If loyalty measures behavior, equity measures attitudes. Properly balanced, loyalty should enhance equity and equity should drive loyalty. But loyalty and equity are not the same thing.

Fans are immensely loyal to sports teams without having to be bribed, because sports teams have equity. Or consider political parties. If you're like most people, you've been a member of the same political party for years. You almost always vote for its candidates, you might have donated money to it, and you may have even volunteered your precious time—yes, for free. Political parties have equity.

Now make a mental list of your favorite brands. You pay more for them, go out of your way to acquire them, and recommend them to your friends—all for free. Every brand has some level of equity, but some have more than others. And the key to boosting equity is to increase affection—the feeling that drives behavior rather than just the behavior itself.

Many companies have gone too far down the road of focusing on loyalty at the expense of equity. I'm so afraid of forgetting about or losing the rewards I've "earned" that it's just one more burden I have to deal with. But affection is always positive.

So-called loyalty can be bought. Equity must be earned. And equity is the only thing that remains after the points and perks expire.

45
DISCOUNTING IS DANGEROUS

AS A MARKETER WHOSE PASSION IS CREATING PREFERENCE AND profitability for the brands with which I work, I don't like discounting. In fact, I hate it. It's distracting. It's demeaning. It's destructive and depressing. And yet I see companies embrace it all the time.

Even brands that should know better—those that have made big bets on discounting in the past and lost—have not been immune. After a brief flirtation with trying to turn its slow decline around through a bold rebranding effort, in 2013 J.C. Penney fired its high-profile CEO, Ron Johnson, and went right back to the slow-death discounting game.

Discounting destroys brand equity, hamstrings investment in innovation, and zaps profitability for companies and their stakeholders. J.C. Penney's move—and others like it that get made in boardrooms every day—raises an interesting question: Can discounting *ever* be an acceptable strategy for a business?

The answer, of course, is yes. There are times and places where a discount can make sense to achieve a limited, well-defined objective. That said, discounting should be used rarely and managed carefully. Let me suggest three rules of thumb that should be kept in mind if (when) you begin flirting with the beast.

First: Discount briefly. Discounting is like a drug. Employed for a limited time to treat a specific condition, it can have its place. But like a drug, discounting is addictive. Brands that get hooked on it do little more than drive their value proposition down, sometimes past the point of no return.

This is one reason why department stores constantly fluctuate between growth and decline, launching Red Tag sales as soon as their Red Apple sales are over. They discount so often that they train customers not to shop if there isn't a sale going on. (My firm even produced a campaign for a retail client that spoofed how department stores would look for just about any reason to discount, such as the "Life's Not Fair Sale" and "President Polk Day Sale.")

Second: Discount credibly. Handled carefully, discounting can be used to achieve specific business objectives without compromising your brand's overall value perception. The key is to make the rationale behind the discount credible (and obvious) to consumers, so they don't perceive it as an act of desperation.

For instance, Apple's student discount on laptops doesn't damage the brand because it's based on a rational corporate reason (get young computer users hooked on its products) and a credible consumer need (students are poor). The company also offers 10 percent off a new iPod when customers recycle their old one, which not only encourages upgrading but also makes Apple look like a responsible corporate citizen. Both of these tactics enable Apple to maintain (perhaps even increase) brand equity while making its products more accessible.

Beware the rush that discounting brings; it's easy to get hooked.

Third: Discount creatively. Wise brands understand that price is just one element of the value equation and find ways to "discount without discounting" by focusing on other elements of the marketing mix. Luxury leather goods maker Coach did just that by adjusting its merchandise inventory so that half of its handbags would be regularly priced between $200 and $300 (compared to its historical average price of $325). While this move may still have some negative impact on the long-term equity of the Coach brand name, it's less damaging than hanging a "30% off" tag from the handle of every purse.

Or consider video game retailer GameStop, which during tough economic times pushes the sales of used games that have a naturally lower price point. That keeps customers in the habit of coming to its stores to find what they want. Rather than hurting its future pricing power by discounting new merchandise, the brand has found another way to satisfy its customers in the short term.

The bottom line: In your customers' eyes, your product is either worth regular price or it's not. If your value equation doesn't add up in their minds, you should focus on finding a way to make it do so without reflexively taking a percentage off the top. If you do choose to incorporate discounting into your strategy, it must appear sensible and smart, not irrational or a result of panic.

People understand that prices are a market mechanism. If you start playing the discount card too much, you're sending a signal that you don't believe your brand is worth the price. And if you don't believe it, who will?

WHERE AND WHEN

YOU KNOW WHO. YOU KNOW WHAT. AND YOU KNOW HOW. NOW comes the hard part, believe it or not. No matter how good the plan, the where and when of your efforts will determine the fate of your brand.

46

CONVERGENCE SPELLS OPPORTUNITY

HEAR SOMEONE MENTION "CAR" AND "CULT" IN THE SAME SEN-tence, and it's likely they'll be talking about the Mini Cooper. Since its original launch in 1959, Mini has attracted the attention of fun-seekers the world over because of its shape, size, zip, and quirky personality.

The Mini Cooper won the Monte Carlo Rally a handful of times in the mid-1960s, and Mini sold some 10,000 vehicles in America that decade before new government safety and emissions regulations forced the brand to withdraw from the U.S. market.[1]

Enter BMW, which bought Mini and relaunched it in 2001, achieving annual sales of a million units within seven short years.[2] Mini quickly became a global success story despite being heavily outspent by its closest competitors. How? From the beginning, the brain trust at Mini recognized a convergence of the worlds of journalism and market-ing. That spelled opportunity.

The world of journalism isn't what it used to be. Thinly disguised promotional tactics are on the rise—you need no more evidence of this than when the teaser for your late local news just happens to feature a story tied to the topic of the prime-time show leading into it. There are more cable channels, more radio channels, more magazines, and infi-nitely more Web sites, blogs, and other online avenues competing for valuable content.

That alone would be difficult for journalists to contend with, let alone the fact that newsrooms are shrinking even as their task of finding original, compelling, and unique stories is getting more difficult. The news business abhors a vacuum as much as nature does. That "news hole" presents a window of opportunity for a captivating narrative—especially one with pictures. The fact that a brand may be behind it is increasingly acceptable.

Enter Mini. Not only did the brand know who it was targeting and what its brand was about, it knew that "earned" media could greatly extend the reach of its limited budget. In keeping with its fun persona, Mini pulled a handful of photogenic stunts, then provided the evidence to the media. The brand story spread from there.

When Mini relaunched in the United States, for example, newspapers, television stations and websites the world over picked up an image of the cute little car getting a piggyback ride atop a Chevy Suburban sporting a banner that said "What are you doing for fun this weekend?" The stunt cost next to nothing to pull off, in auto marketing terms.

> **The lines between journalism, advertising, and entertainment are increasingly blurred.**

Mini pulled a similar stunt around Christmastime in Amsterdam, leaving a handful of giant, open cardboard boxes, with tissue paper and ribbons spilling over the sides, on corner trash piles. The boxes had a UPC code and an image of the Mini Cooper on the side, as if the car came in a box like any other toy to delight those who found one under the tree on Christmas morning. It was a charming photo (and video) opportunity, and it was seen all over the world—despite the fact that the boxes were staged in only 12 locations.[3]

Simple stunts. Big impacts. Both leveraging the trend toward convergence.

As the lines between marketing and journalism (and for that matter, entertainment) continue to blur, it will become increasingly difficult to recognize where one ends and the other begins. The better you understand what's happening, the more your brand can benefit from it. It doesn't cost a lot of money, and it need not take a lot of time. All it takes is imagination.

47
BRANDING IS EVERYTHING

I RECALL A CROSS-COUNTRY PLANE RIDE DURING WHICH MY CO-passengers and I enjoyed the humor of a funny flight attendant. We were in stitches as he delivered the safety briefing with the wit and timing of a stand-up comedian, and when we prepared for landing, he was just as hilarious.

As enjoyable as the experience was, I've come to expect that type of lighthearted humor from Southwest Airlines. And as we were taxiing toward the gate, I reflected on my appreciation of the company's attempts to make traveling just a little less of a hassle. But then I realized something. I was on an American Airlines flight.

Think about that. I made my reservation at the American Airlines Web site. I checked in at the American Airlines ticket counter. I waited at the American Airlines gate, handed my ticket to the American Airlines agent, stepped on to the American Airlines plane, and slumped into an American Airlines seat, with the American Airlines in-flight magazine staring back from the seat-back pocket in front of me. Yet despite all that, the wit and charm of the flight attendant was so consistent with brand Southwest (and, frankly, inconsistent with American) that it had me subconsciously thinking that I was on a different airline.

Is it possible that the freedom Southwest has long given its flight attendants to improvise has made the lighthearted safety briefing an asset of its brand? How often when the other guys mimic the approach does it result in an unintentional tip of the hat to Southwest? Whether intended or not, Southwest now owns the funny flight briefing in my mind, and I suspect in the minds of many others. Southwest understands that everything it does has an impact on its brand.

Year after year, Southwest's competitors try to take advantage of the fact that the airline doesn't assign seats and serves its customers tiny bags of peanuts. The other airlines actually see these as negative elements of the Southwest customer experience.

What they don't understand is that to Southwest customers, lining up for a seat and nibbling peanuts actually enhances their image of the brand. Even though lines and cheap snacks aren't positive experiences in themselves, they reinforce the primary reason why people choose to fly Southwest: to save a buck. Southwest doesn't choose what it serves only because of the cost but because it bolsters the image of what customers think they pay: peanuts. And delivering it all with a smile (as Southwest does so consistently) makes it more than tolerable.

Since its founding as "the LUV airline," Southwest has consistently nurtured its brand internally as well, to the point that it's now part of the company's DNA. Like-minded people want to work for Southwest, and the company has earned the luxury of being able to screen applicants carefully to ensure a good fit. That makes even Southwest's corporate culture part of its brand.

> **Branding isn't just what you do. It's who you are.**

Too many CEOs believe branding is a discipline that lives in the marketing department. But branding is everything a company does, from the logo on its letterhead, to the way it handles customer complaints, to whether its uniformed personnel keep their shirts tucked in. (The latter is a challenge a current client of my firm is facing.) Company leaders who ignore this do so at their peril.

The other night, my wife and I decided to try a new restaurant we had heard about. But when we pulled up to the entrance we just kept on driving, never even getting out of the car. It was the restaurant's sign that gave us pause. It was simply a flat, translucent panel with an amateurish, one-color vinyl logo slapped on—the kind of sign you would see on a check-cashing operation in a seedy strip mall. The sign was of low quality and in bad taste—imagery not well associated with a fine-dining establishment. With plenty of other good choices, we simply didn't want to take the risk of spoiling our dinner date.

For all I know, the food would have been amazing and the chef an undiscovered gem, but the restaurant never got the chance to prove it because we naturally assumed the experience would be as unprofessional as the sign.

Perhaps after a few more quiet weekends the proprietor will realize that branding is everything and will do something about the sign. Perhaps not. But contrast that with an experience a colleague recently had after she purchased a new pair of running shoes.

Not only did she enjoy a positive experience in the store, a few days later she received a call from a pleasant customer-service representative who simply wanted to ensure everything was still okay. That impressed her. Shortly thereafter, the store, unprompted, delivered a handy gym bag to thank her for her business. Needless to say, she now considers herself "in the club" and is telling everyone she knows about it. And there wasn't an ad or Web site in the mix.

When you think about branding, it's easy to limit your perspective to the verbal and visual expressions you put into the marketplace. But there isn't anything that anybody within your organization does (or fails to do) that doesn't affect at some level how your brand is perceived.

48
CREDIBILITY IS CRITICAL

WHAT MAKES BRANDS LIKE MINI AND SOUTHWEST AIRLINES SO powerful is the incredible top-to-bottom consistency they exhibit in everything they do. While no brand or organization is perfect, these two are among the leaders of the pack.

So is Mini's parent company, BMW. For one, it recognized that while Mini's association with the iconic parent brand would be a credibility builder, it wisely stopped short of plastering the BMW logo all over everything Mini. A brand that works great for one target audience doesn't necessarily work well for another, and sometimes you can stretch a brand so thin that it rips. BMW understands that.

Listen to what longtime marketing chief Jim McDowell says about the credibility of his brand. "Everything we do is about strengthening the brand. . . . A BMW is the 'Ultimate Driving Machine.' We've interpreted it in different ways and demonstrated it through different models, but that fundamental idea has never varied. If you want to be really vivid with precise edges in the marketplace, you have to have the discipline to prune away relentlessly all the things that you're not. Few marketers have this discipline. We can all name the ones who do. And their brands are famous, trusted, and reliable."

Credibility is critical in branding. No matter how good your brand appears on the surface, sooner or later it's going to get scratched—you'll ship a product that's a lemon, deliver an unacceptable service experience, or offend a customer who's having a bad hair day. If the scratch reveals that underneath the surface is more of the same, you'll be able to recover. If it exposes your brand as mere veneer, however, you're going to get called on it.

One time I was at the Southwest ticket counter checking my bags, and I ran into a particularly nasty agent that put a scratch in the airline's brand. She seemed angry with me for simply being there and scolded me for no apparent reason as she rushed me along. There were no long lines, I wasn't late for my flight—I simply offended her by showing up. Or maybe she just had indigestion.

As I reflected about my experience on the way through security, I noticed how I was interpreting the event differently than I would have if she had worked for another airline. In that case it would have been easy to count the bad experience as one more example of how legacy airlines don't give a rip about their customers. I know I'm overstating it a bit, but I have come to expect poor treatment from those brands (hey, at least they're consistent).

> **Contradictions kill credibility.**

In this case, however, I not only gave Southwest a pass, I actually felt sorry for the brand. One of its own was behaving in a way that hurt it, and I didn't want that to happen. Southwest has been such a friend over the years that the space the brand occupies in my brain simply rejected this one example of rude behavior. Not only did that one bad experience do no damage, in an odd way it may have enhanced the brand by making me consider why I reacted the way I did. If it happens again soon I may start to reconsider, but for me this experience served as an exception that proved the rule.

Branding often gets a bad rap for being manipulative. But manipulators can't keep up their ruse for long, and once they're exposed, the game is up. Brands that want to be lasting can't risk that, and great brands don't. They focus relentlessly on delivering on their brand ideas and prune away everything that puts them at risk.

49
SALES AND MARKETING MIX

IF BRANDING IS EVERYTHING AND CREDIBILITY IS CRITICAL, there may be no more common place where things tend to break down than the sales-versus-marketing divide.

The problem is as insidious as it is old. Sales professionals have historically dismissed marketers as lightweights who make things look pretty; marketers tend to look down their noses at sales Neanderthals who wouldn't recognize good taste if it hit them in the mouth. This is why at many companies, sales and marketing departments simply coexist. It ought not be that way.

Customers these days are too mobile, too connected, and too informed to tolerate any gap between what one department says and another does. This means that brands intending to succeed can't allow sales and marketing to operate in different spheres.

One of the last places you might expect to find leading-edge practices in this regard is in a fashion brand like Burberry. The brand, famous for trench coats, plaids, and gabardine, is more than 150 years old and has had many periods of ups and downs. But Burberry has seen double-digit sales growth under the watchful eye of CEO Angela Ahrendts.[1]

Styling, of course, is key, but behind the scenes, Burberry uses sophisticated CRM software to analyze what customers are doing across social media and within diverse sales channels—in-store, desktop, tablet, and mobile. The brand recognizes that the so-called line between sales and marketing is an anachronism.

For most consumers, buying fashion clothing and accessories is fun. So is buying a computer. It wasn't always that way, however. Buying a computer used to be as confusing and distasteful as buying a car, but the experience has evolved into something much more pleasant. Why the difference?

In the automotive world, sales and marketing have always been segregated; different companies with different priorities and differing cultures drive the buying experience. That's the way it used to be in the computer industry too, until big manufacturers like Apple and Microsoft got into the retail game. They've been able to integrate from factory to showroom floor to the point where you can't really tell where marketing ends and sales begins. That reflects a sea change in customer expectations—one to which every industry ought to be paying attention.

> **Divide and be conquered.**

Unfortunately, such examples are rare, particularly when it comes to brands with limited resources. But even small restaurants intuitively understand it. What fine-dining establishment would invest in décor, furniture, menus, heat, light, point-of-sale systems, advertising, and everything else while neglecting the waitstaff who have the most influence on customer satisfaction? Equally ridiculous would be to expect waiters to satisfy customers in a musty warehouse where food arrives by conveyor belt. Restaurateurs know what computer makers and fashion brands have come to understand and the rest of the world is now awakening to: Customer retention, client referrals, and profit margins can all be enhanced when sales and marketing are fully aligned.

It's crucial that salespeople view marketing not as a department but as a philosophy: Prospects must be nurtured through the early stages of attraction and engagement before they'll be willing to close a deal. Marketers must similarly understand that sales is not merely a function or department but the brand's ear to the ground and the point where all that brand equity is realized in a transaction. It's where the game is won.

The two disciplines should not only be above conflict, they should be joined at the hip. The sales perspective must be woven into and throughout an organization's integrated marketing program, with marketing philosophy informing everything that sales does.

Automakers may not have a lot of options in this arena, but you do. If you have a divide between sales and marketing, bridge it. Cross-train the two disciplines, ensure that they have access to the same data, make them responsible for each other's metrics, and set expectations regarding collaboration. Seat them side by side, if you must. It doesn't matter whether marketing reports to sales or sales reports to marketing, as long as everybody involved understands the purpose, power, and possibilities of both.

Bridging the sales-versus-marketing divide is crucial to building an effective integrated marketing program. Doing so may require a change in perspective, but it will build equity for your brand as well as for those who buy it.

50
INTEGRATION IS POWER

IF IT AIN'T BROKE, DON'T FIX IT IS SUCH A CLICHÉ THAT IT HAS spawned its own cliché: If it ain't broke, break it. Unfortunately, that's just what many brands unwittingly do, playing into the hands of public enemy number one in today's marketing environment: fragmentation.

As we've acknowledged, more and more television networks, radio stations, and print titles are competing for attention, and new marketing channels pop up every day, from apps to social networks and beyond. The number of places we hit people with marketing messages is growing a lot faster than the number of eyeballs that can take them in, and as a result, audiences (and attention spans) are becoming increasingly fragmented. That reduces the chance any message has of getting through.

Even sales channels are fragmenting beyond the online-versus-bricks-and-mortar divide to which we've become somewhat accustomed. Desktop and laptop purchases are giving way to shopping via smartphone—at a time when many companies don't even have a mobile Web site, to say nothing of e-commerce capabilities. Add inflation to the mix (even with miniscule increases, the wonder of compounding is working against you), and fragmentation can shred what once was a healthy marketing budget.

The good news is that there is a powerful way to overcome fragmentation: integration. But it's more difficult than it appears.

Integration is not simply slapping a common tagline onto all your ads, using a single color palette, or force-fitting a message that's suited for one medium into another (great television commercials rarely translate well to outdoor billboards, which in turn are very different from online banners).

Integration means communicating a consistent identity from message to message, and medium to medium, and (more important) delivering consistently on that identity. It requires not only the identification of a powerful, unifying strategy and compelling voice for your brand but the discipline to roll it into every aspect of your organization—from advertising to sales, customer service to customer relationship management programs and beyond. Remember, branding is everything.

When ice cream maker Häagen-Dazs wanted to raise awareness about the mysterious decline in the North American honey bee population, it launched an integrated campaign featuring not only television commercials, print ads, and magazine inserts but an online microsite, YouTube videos, tie-ins with important retailers, and even a new flavor, Vanilla Honey Bee, the profits of which were donated to honey bee research. A PR campaign wrapped the advertising and promotional efforts in a nice package for the press, leading many major media outlets to pick up the story. Just one week after launch, the campaign generated more than 125 million PR impressions, and Häagen-Dazs was even called to testify on the bees' behalf before the U.S. Senate Agricultural Subcommittee.[1]

> **Integration is the cure for fragmentation.**

Even with that effort, Häagen-Dazs only scratched the surface of what's possible with a deep commitment to integration. All that you do to attract, convert, retain, and engage your customers can be integrated. If your brand isn't woven beyond your marketing efforts into your human resource practices, your training programs, even your compensation and employee evaluation metrics, you're leaving opportunity on the table. You're also risking backlash, as spurned or burned customers take to social media to make their complaints heard. It's vital to deliver consistent signals in everything you do.

That raises a question: If fragmentation is so damaging and integration such a powerful counterforce, why don't brands implement an integration strategy more often? It's not for lack of understanding, desire, or even intent in the minds of most marketers. It's for lack of perseverance.

Put simply, integration takes time. It's not easy to integrate a brand into a wide suite of processes, materials, and messages that have been shepherded by different people, driven by different objectives, and brought to life in different places within the organization. Many brands simply don't have the patience to see it through.

Find a time to gather together as many different expressions of what your brand says and does in one place, then make an honest evaluation. If it doesn't all connect for you in some meaningful fashion, it won't for your customers and prospects either.

If your strategy is weak or off the mark, you may need to reexamine your who or your what. But it may be that your problem is more a matter of execution—your what and where. If so, your enemy is entropy: Everything in the universe (including your brand) tends toward disarray, and in that case your role is to be gravity. No one else is going to hold it all together.

Not so long ago, it was enough to have great strategy and a big idea. Today, even the best ideas have a hard time getting off the ground as consumers' media and purchasing options—not to mention their attention spans—grow increasingly fragmented. While perfect integration may be unachievable, brands that do the best job of harmonizing all their efforts have an advantage.

51

SOCIAL CAN BE SLIPPERY

WHEN IT FIRST CAME ON THE SCENE, SOCIAL MEDIA WAS CONSIDered a luxury (or distraction), but it has since proved its chops. Smart brands have come to recognize it not as a project, initiative, or even a department but as a way of doing business.

Too often the way companies approach social media is similar to how people approach dieting: Initial excitement soon turns to discouragement and ultimately disillusionment. Success in either area begins with strategy; you can increase the odds of achieving your goals by thinking ahead and customizing an approach that works for your specific situation.

One strategic mistake many brands make is choosing social media platforms based on what they are comfortable with as consumers. That's like advertising in a fly-fishing magazine simply because you're a fly fisherman—it might be the right decision, but not if you run a bakery. You need to take into account the characteristics of your brand, the profile of your audience, the nature of your message, and the strengths and weaknesses of each platform before you can prioritize where to focus your efforts.

Another common mistake is jumping onto multiple platforms without taking time to understand them. Each social media ecosystem has its own subculture, language, rhythm, and rules, all of which must be fully mastered to generate success. You can't fake it or take shortcuts; brands that, for example, dump identical content on different platforms just look obtuse. If you don't have a good grasp of the peculiarities of each social media platform you choose, you should think twice before jumping onto it.

One reality that's often overlooked when brands skip the strategy step is the never-ending need for new content. Social media is a river that runs 24/7, and once you establish a presence, it's vital to keep paddling. Brands that don't determine a thoughtful and scalable content development strategy ahead of time can easily find themselves watching the conversation flow by.

Establishing what you want to accomplish, what it's going to require, and how you intend to go about it will enable you to determine what metrics you'll need to measure success, another often-overlooked step. Big brands have the bucks to develop customized systems for information gathering and analysis. You may not, but dozens of affordable Web-based services can get you most of the way there. As your program grows, the metrics you set up (based on your strategy and tied to your objectives) should justify allocating the budgets and staff time necessary to enlarge your social presence.

> **Misunderstand social media and your brand will be misunderstood.**

The heaviest (and frequently underestimated) lifting is designing and installing the processes you'll need to effectively allocate your limited time and budget resources. Somebody needs to be in charge of trend watching, content development, calendar creation, writing, editing, posting, interacting, responding (in as close to real time as possible), and, depending on the platforms used, photography, graphic design, video production, and more. It can get hairy fast.

Even if you're starting small, say with a presence on a single social media site, you mustn't underestimate the time required to be effective. The biggest time sink: content creation. It takes even more time if a blog is a part of your strategy.

This isn't meant to intimidate you. As your social media program grows, there are outsourcing options for every element. The best tasks on which to spend your limited vendor dollars: strategy development and process design. Best practices are rapidly emerging in these areas (thus no need for you to reinvent the wheel), and a professional partner can tailor them to the realities of your specific goals and capabilities.

Content development is another area that often can be outsourced, as long as the handoff (turning that content into actual posts) is well managed. But the one thing you shouldn't outsource is your brand voice. Social media is not just about what you say but how you say it. The whole point is generating real-time conversation and responding as events unfold. That's just not something you want to vend.

In the not-too-distant future, there will really be no way to separate social media from the rest of the enterprise—it can or will affect not only marketing but customer service, accounting, research, investor relations, vendor relationships, distribution, and even product design. Getting a jump on managing it well now can give nimble brands the ability to get out in front of slower competitors.

52
DATA IS BIG

HERE'S A NUMBER YOU DON'T HEAR EVERY DAY: A QUINTILLION. That's a 1 followed by 18 zeroes; a billion billion; a million trillion. As immense as a quintillion is, IBM reports that each day—every day—the world creates 2.5 quintillion bytes of new data. By comparison, all of the earth's oceans contain just 352 quintillion gallons of water; if bytes were buckets, it would take only about 20 weeks of information gathering to fill the seas.

We're swimming in so much data it threatens to drown us. That's not a bad metaphor, actually. As any swimmer can tell you, if you flail and fight the water, it will take you down. But if you relax and work with it, the water will hold you up.

Data in and of itself is of no use if it's not in a form that can be easily accessed and understood. But as software increasingly allows for better collecting, sifting, and sorting—turning data into information and information into insight—data can offer extreme competitive advantages.

Broadly speaking, data offers three big benefits. The first is in helping a brand understand what has happened in the past, be it measured in years, months, or minutes. Every brand can benefit from a better understanding of where its customers come from, why they do what they do, and how they might be better served, and this information can increasingly be gleaned quickly, accurately, and in fine detail.

For example, my firm conducted an analysis using data visualization software that correlated one brand's media spending, Web traffic, customer inquiries, and purchase activity to discover the relative relationships between each of those metrics. We also tracked overall results to increases or decreases in advertising spending as well as the effects of lag time in between media buys. That understanding proved invaluable in leveraging the second big benefit of data, instantaneous response.

From hospitals predicting demand for beds by tracking flu-related search queries to online retailers adjusting to fluctuating demand by changing prices of products on a minute-by-minute basis, data well utilized can have real-time impact. Accurate data helps brands make adjustments to their ad campaigns on the fly, letting actual consumer behavior drive changes rather than relying on syndicated research, predictive models, or intuition. With access to the right information, a brand can turn on a dime to adjust in a continually changing environment.

Data can also have a significant impact on customer satisfaction. Ryan Hollenbeck, senior vice president of marketing at Verint Systems, a workforce optimization and analytics technology company based in Melville, New York, shared with me the story of a brand that set up a "listening post" in its contact center and used software to look for patterns in customer conversations. The brand discovered (to its horror) that it was unintentionally misleading some customers with its advertising.

> **The more there is to know, the more you need to know it.**

Another brand used speech analytics to analyze the conversations of customers who were terminating their accounts, then used key words and phrases to identify other at-risk customers. Reaching out to these at-risk customers, the brand reported that it saved some 600 accounts and more than $12 million in revenue in the first year of the program.

As powerful as that is, perhaps the most exciting application of data is in helping brands anticipate the future. Just as police departments are increasingly using data to predict where and when crimes may happen, forward-thinking brands are using customers' behavioral data to project how new products will perform among their existing customer bases.

And whereas the initial promise of social media appeared to lie in brands' ability to interact with their fans in real time, its bigger value may lie in analyzing gigabytes of conversations to determine customer sentiment, identify product improvements, head off nascent public relations crises, and understand evolving consumer needs and perceptions. As Hollenbeck puts it, "The conversation and dialogue that takes place on social mediums may very well translate into a tremendous potential focus group."

The rise of the online economy has changed the way brands relate to their customers. Decades ago, when most business was conducted face-to-face, companies could get to know their customers in a personal way. But today, leisurely conversations are being replaced by instantaneous connections.

If you're not already doing so, spend a few bucks plumbing the depths of your data. The confidence you gain from seeing returns on your investment will enable you to take increasingly deeper dives.

53

CRM CAN BACKFIRE

COMBINING THE EFFICIENCY OF DATA UTILIZATION WITH THE EF-
ficacy of social media is a powerful proposition. And that is, in fact,
where customer relationship management (CRM) programs are headed.
These are exciting times that offer significant opportunities for alert and
responsive brands. But great care must be taken not to let CRM overstep
the bounds of polite branding.

Traditional CRM programs have delivered significant value to
brands that have embraced them. They've lowered costs and enhanced
profitability, providing customers with custom offers, product recom-
mendations, timely resolutions to their complaints, and other rewards
of data sharing. But there have also been notable downsides to CRM
that have made it, according to my colleague Emily Griebel, "like an
acronym for a disease."

Haven't we all experienced times when poorly executed CRM programs have made us a bit nauseous? Sometimes you could swear CRM
means customer relationship *manipulation,* such as when too-clever
brands print customers' names on postcards as if to fool them into
thinking they were personally addressed. I smirk when I receive a mailer
that says "Just for you, Stephen" or something similarly smarmy. Nobody
calls me Stephen, other than my mother (and only when she's angry).
It's even funnier when it's addressed to Stphn Mrkey or some other
butchered version of the name with which I was christened.

Other times you'd think CRM means customer relationship *mini-
mization.* That's never so much in evidence than with "telephone trees."
Tone-deaf brands love them, but I've never met a human who doesn't

view them with contempt. Telephone trees lower costs, to be sure, but they do so on the backs of customers who are forced to navigate their way through a frustrating forest of options, only to end up at a dead end or repeatedly entering their account number because the customer service system isn't compatible with the customer complaint system, which itself isn't compatible with the customer service person speaking broken English who finally comes on the line after you pound "0" repeatedly and scream "AGENT!" into the receiver 17 times.

Sometimes CRM seems to refer to customer relationship *mechanization*. You may appreciate Amazon making suggestions based on your reading interests, but the fact that you bought a baby book for a friend doesn't mean you're pregnant (yes, that really happened to an associate of mine).

Perhaps most stomach turning is when CRM refers to cold, hard customer relationship *monetization*. A few years ago I was struck by the number of mailers I was receiving from the various divisions of a large credit card company, so I decided to collect them. I found that I was receiving an average of three to five per week—an annoyance to me and an immense waste of money for them. And in the past year alone, one of my favorite brands has emailed me 105 times (I've been counting). I'm sure the content and frequency of emails is somehow based on my purchase activity (or lack thereof), but it comes across as insensitive and somewhat desperate. Good customers want to be courted, not cashed in on, and courtship requires careful pacing and rhythm.

> **Relationships should be nurtured, not managed.**

That's the thing traditional CRM systems don't account for well. Customer relationships aren't built on information, they're built on trust. When one party focuses too much on acquiring and leveraging information, trust can't help but be compromised, if not breached. The problem with traditional CRM is that it turns people into data and relationships into rules of engagement. But technology has no empathy, and a database will never be as responsive as a living, breathing person.

That's why social media is of such keen interest to CRM companies. Two-thirds of American consumers use social networking sites, and they're talking 24/7 about great service and insolent reps, smart branding and shameless attempts at manipulation. The data (and the power) is increasingly in their hands, representing a 180-degree pivot from traditional CRM. That has added a whole new dimension to the term: CRM could now just as easily be called *company* relationship management. I think that's healthy.

For decades, CRM has been one-sided, and that has produced a variety of maladies beyond even the ones I mentioned above. Now that social media is enabling company relationship management, the delicate balance of trust between brands and their customers can be better maintained. It's one big step in the direction of relationship equilibrium, and that will be good for both sides.

If you've been pondering how best to use CRM for your brand, you may want to begin with where it's going rather than where it has been. Start by listening rather than talking, responding rather than pitching. The best brands have always understood that by focusing on relationships, customers will manage themselves.

54

ANALOG IS AWESOME

YOU WOULD HAVE THOUGHT THAT WITH THE ADVENT OF THE COM-
pact disc and the clarity and consistency digital music provides, turn-
tables and needles would by now have disappeared, making all those
record albums stored in your garage worthless. But you may want to
think twice before you pitch them in the trash or trade a stack for a large
pizza (an act of which I am guilty and now regret).

For instance, if you happen to have a 1963 copy of *The Freewheelin'
Bob Dylan*, featuring four tracks that were deleted from subsequent releases, it would fetch you some $35,000. And the Beatles' 1966 *Yesterday
and Today* album in a butcher sleeve would net you nearly $40,000.[1]
Don't get too excited—most of your old LPs are likely worth just pen-
nies. But some could net you $5, $10, or even $50 if you took the time
to sort and sell them. As record collector Bill Cox puts it, "Vinyl is a
different breed of passion."[2]

In our increasingly digital world, analog can offer a refreshing
change. I recently toured Austin-based Quantum Digital, a company
that integrates digital technologies with direct mail, print, online, and
mobile to optimize consumer response. The operation is impressive and
filled with the quiet purr of the latest high-tech digital printing, routing,
and shipping machines.

What I found most impressive during the tour, however, was the
reception desk. Eric Cosway, EVP/CMO (and our tour guide), introduced us to a charming woman who sat there and proudly announced
that when you call Quantum Digital, you will always speak with a real
person.

I applaud the decision by a company with digital DNA to recognize when an analog solution is still best. Too many companies these days are enamored with the efficiency and cost savings of those awful telephone trees. Those of us on the other end know that what it really represents is a way to transfer costs and inefficiencies to us.

There's nothing wrong with automation and digitization. But the more brands automate and digitize, the less personal their efforts tend to be. Who hasn't received correspondence from a brand with a preprinted greeting and digitized signature that makes the pretense of being personal? The intention may be good, but the execution leaves a lot to be desired and can, in fact, leave an impression counter to what the brand intends.

Just because it can be done digitally doesn't mean it should be.

On my desk right now is a catalog (sent to tens of thousands of companies, no doubt) that boasts of "Cards & Calendars Designed with Your Business in Mind." Never mind that they've never even heard of my business. It tells me that if I make a purchase of $250 or more, I'll receive a free gift. They hope to make expressing my sentiments easy, convenient, and financially rewarding.

Perhaps the catalog frames the problem better than anything. Not only does it offer me faux-personal ways to express non-heartfelt feelings to unappreciative customers, it does so in a faux-personal way to me. It's a lie from the cover on.

Reaching inboxes and mailboxes is easy. Reaching hearts and minds is more difficult. When it's time for your brand to say thank you, happy birthday, or express any other personal sentiment to your customers, vendors, prospects, and employees, don't be hypnotized by the promise of efficiency. Find a way to make the expression sincere, heartfelt, and personal.

55
INVESTING RETURNS

IN THE TEETH OF THE 2009 RECESSION, DR PEPPER SNAPPLE Group made a bold decision to increase its $350 million marketing budget. At the time Jim Trebilcock, executive VP of marketing at the company, said in an *Ad Age* interview that the company looked at what happened during the deep recession of the 1980s and found that the packaged goods brands that were most successful coming out of the downturn were those that invested in their brands throughout.

Said Trebilcock, "We have, in our portfolio, a host of brands that are very trusted, high-quality brands. And at times like these, we believe if we invest in them . . . we can make a pretty significant impact on our business moving forward and actually strengthen and position ourselves for consistent growth when we come out of this economic downturn."[1] Sure enough, the following year, Dr Pepper Snapple Group's market share grew 4 percent, while Coca-Cola's and PepsiCo's both declined.[2]

Invest more, get more. It's a general principle of branding. But how much is too much? More importantly, how much is enough? While there is no definitive answer, there are general guidelines any brand can use to develop a formula that works.

As a first step, you might want to determine what other brands in your industry spend. Public companies may provide the figure in their financial statements, and with a simple calculation you can figure out what percentage of their overall revenue that represents. If you can't find any good comparative information, you might want to start at 5 percent and then adjust your projected spending up or down based on the objectives of your brand, the size of your market, the cost of media, and the speed at which you'd like to grow. You'll also need to ask yourself if your brand is built on volume or margin. Even within industries, there are substantial differences in the marketing spend of volume-driven brands compared with margin-driven ones.

Volume-driven brands tend to spend a tiny percentage of sales on marketing, in part because their large revenues enable small contributions to add up fast and in part because of the margin pressures they face in having to compete with other high-volume brands. By contrast, margin-driven brands tend to spend a larger percentage of sales on marketing: They have room in their margins to afford it, and they're often working from a smaller revenue base.

The retail industry provides some good examples. While Walmart might spend a meager 0.4 percent of sales on advertising, the sheer size of the company turns that tiny percentage into a significant budget. Walmart's nominally higher-margin competitor, Target, spends closer to 2 percent of its sales on advertising, while Best Buy, as a specialty retailer, spends upward of 3 percent. Finally, more upscale stores like Macy's typically spend on the order of 5 percent.

Branding is an investment, not an expense.

The same kind of ratios can be seen in the car industry (automakers' generally spend 2.5 to 3.5 percent of revenue on marketing), packaged goods (4 to 10 percent), and every other industry.

If you're in a services business, you might want to bump your starting point higher than 5 percent. For example, like most professional services firms, my company is more margin oriented than volume oriented, so fueling its growth requires that we spend a higher percentage of our revenues. I've seen some margin-driven brands spend upward of 15 percent when warranted—especially young brands that need to invest to build equity.

It's important to make a qualification here. Giant consumer brands such as automakers, packaged-food manufacturers, and retail chains spend a huge percentage of their marketing dollars on paid media advertising, the most visible (and expensive) tool in the marketing toolbox.

Depending on the size of your brand and the business you're in, advertising might not be the right (and certainly not the only) tool for you.

The important thing is intentionally and deliberately to set aside some rational percentage of your revenue to get out there. That way, the question you have to answer isn't "How much should we spend?" but rather "How do we spend most effectively?"

As in the financial markets, some investments will do better than others. Don't expect to hit it out of the park every time; just make sure you budget enough times at bat. If you've developed your who, what, and how effectively, the return on your investment in when and where will continue to grow.

56
ROI MAY BE DECEIVING

ROI IS THE BUZZ THESE DAYS. NOT THAT IT HASN'T ALWAYS BEEN important, but with the advent of online marketing and the data it generates, the prospects of being able to measure the return on branding investment is better than ever. But you have to be careful not to expect too much from your measurements.

The first client I ever worked with was a big restaurant chain whose CEO was famous in our firm for demanding advertising that "makes the cash register ring." There's nothing to argue with there, of course, and we were determined to do our best to give it to him.

What couldn't escape my notice, however, were all of the things that got between our good intentions and that lovely jingling sound at the end of the transaction. I remember thinking it was a little simplistic to expect advertising to both initiate and complete the sale. Especially when wait times, table cleanliness, product quality, and staff training, among many other things, contributed to (or detracted from) our success. Even back then, I intuitively knew that everything was branding.

Had we been able to run multiple campaigns and control for certain variables, we would have seen their different impact on sales. But running multiple campaigns wasn't practical (especially in pre-Internet days), and there are a nearly infinite number of variables that can impact efficacy, which is one of the intractable nuisances that plagues any form of ROI research.

Ask a financial advisor how much return you could expect on your 401(k) and instead of an answer, you're likely to get a series of questions. Over what time period? Based on what level of risk? With what liquidity requirements? Many factors go into calculating return on a financial investment, and you always get some sort of required-by-law disclaimer about past performance being no guarantee of future results. The same is true of investing in branding.

Beyond being subject to multiple variables, branding investments have another layer of complexity that financial investments do not. When someone invests $10,000 in a company's stock, for example, it's easy to track what the value of that investment is at any given point in time. The market offers a well-defined way to keep score. Not so with a branding investment. Often there's no telling when it will pay off.

In most cases, prospective customers need to be exposed to a variety of messages over a period of time before they can be convinced to give something a try. And in categories where the purchase is higher risk—such as infrequently bought (electronics, appliances) and high-priced (vacations, cars) products and services—the length of time for effectiveness to become manifest may be even longer.

> **Just because you can't measure it doesn't mean it's not real.**

Consulting firm CoreBrand has conducted years of research about the long-term effects of marketing investments and concludes that it's rare for even a one-year surge in advertising spending to generate measurable results in image development; while you may see a reasonably quick bump in some measurable results, it's usually at least three years before you realize the investment's full effects.[1] As the world of marketing metrics becomes increasingly oriented toward instant gratification, it will be easier to make a short-term decision that's not in your long-term interests.

But that doesn't mean there's nothing you can't effectively track. One significant way to reduce measurement error is to measure ever-smaller things—the steps along the way to a sale rather than the giant leap from awareness to transaction. In the analog world, this involves things like putting a stopwatch on waiting times, mystery shopping to gauge cleanliness and training, and seeding a mailing list with quality-control experts to keep tabs on shipping quality and delivery times. Most brands with a commitment to excellence have some of these measures in place.

It's even easier in the online world to gather impression, activity, and conversion metrics relating to advertising campaigns. What can't be known, however, are how many messages, in what forms of media, that a buyer has been exposed to prior to making a purchase—and that's where the danger arises. There's something deceptively alluring about those online metrics because they look so firm, so final, and so authoritative. But just because they're precise doesn't mean they're correct. Think twice about giving sole credit to the tactic that is identified with the sale.

When it comes to tracking real return on brand investment, by all means gather as much data as you can. But make sure you think globally, considering how other aspects of your comprehensive branding program may be impacting the metrics you're seeing. And be wary—even the best data can be incomplete or at times incorrect. Brands that judge their efforts only by the immediate gratification of easily measured metrics may miss the real story.

Measure ROI in as many ways as you can, in as much detail as you can, and as close to real-time as possible. Just don't confuse metrics with success. They're not always the same thing.

57

ACCRETION IS AMAZING

I CAN'T PUT A METRIC ON HOW MUCH I LOVE MY WIFE, BUT I know it's a whole lot. What's the ROI on vacuuming your store? Of restriping your parking lot? Of being kind to the shipping guy? Of smiling at your employees? As we've seen, just because you can't measure something doesn't mean it's not important. It all adds up.

It's probably not something you've thought about, but the Kool-Aid Man is older than most baby boomers. First brought to life in 1954, the pitch(er)man is currently in his seventh iteration.[1] Kool-Aid's investment in the iconic character continues to pay off, decades after it was first launched. That's the power of brand accretion, and it's something most ROI models don't take into account.

The dictionary defines "accretion" as a process of growth or enlargement by a gradual buildup. With respect to branding, accretion is the simple principle that the more you invest—and the more consistently you invest—the better your long-term returns will be. Everybody accepts the principle of accretion when it comes to real estate, the stock market, and even collectibles. Invest in solid assets, hang on to them, and watch the value of your holdings grow over time. Accretion is the opposite of dilution, something nobody wants—for their balance sheet or their brand.

Unfortunately, many brands neglect the power of accretion. They treat marketing as if it were just another expense, valued only for the benefits it can provide today. That's foolish. Expenses are about immediate gratification—that new-car smell, a high-definition picture, or a faster computer—but the value of those assets declines over time. As we saw in the last chapter, however, investments are different. Investments provide long-term impact that matches and often outweighs their short-term benefits. Investments should be evaluated differently than expenses.

In a branding context, accretion means that none of your efforts exists in a vacuum. Sure, you want those efforts to have an impact today, but they also add to, and are interpreted within, the context of your past and future efforts. Think of branding as a process, not a static point in time; if your message is steady and consistent, you can build significant brand equity. If, however, you continually change your approach, carelessly cut your budget, or seek only short-term benefits, you'll be compromising your own long-term interests.

> **Compounding works as well in branding as it does in investing.**

When I set aside money in my retirement fund, I get some measure of satisfaction that I'm saving for the future, but it's nowhere near the pleasure I'd get from a vacation in the Bahamas. Still, it's a smart thing to do. Brands that judge their efforts only by the immediate gratification of the hits, visits, or sales they quickly generate fail to see the big picture.

Branding is like baseball: You may throw a bad pitch, but it's a long season. If you execute steadily and consistently, the statistics will work in your favor. That's why Anheuser-Busch creates dozens of commercials to determine which six or eight will make the cut to appear during the Super Bowl. It runs the commercials in test markets in the weeks leading up to the game, determining which ones perform best. Those that don't make it aren't a waste of money; they're part of the company's investment in a better final product.

It's likely that your brand has neither the storied history, nor the marketing budget, of Kool-Aid or Anheuser-Busch. That makes the principle of accretion even more important to you. The smaller your brand equity nest egg, the more important it is that you make steady and consistent deposits into it. Any knowledgeable investor knows that changing your investment strategy willy-nilly is ill advised and that every dollar that remains uninvested is a dollar that can't benefit from the power of accretion. The same thing is true for branding.

58
PATIENCE IS A VIRTUE

IN ORDER TO ENJOY THE BENEFITS OF BRAND ACCRETION, IT should go without saying that you need a measure of patience. That isn't always music to a brand manager's ears, especially when aggressive business goals need to be met.

On July 5, 1989, a seminal event in television took place—without anybody knowing it. That was the evening that *The Seinfeld Chronicles* (as it was first known) premiered on NBC. The audience response? Tepid, at best.

NBC wasn't quite sure what to do with *Seinfeld,* and it waffled. The program was then offered to Fox, which took a pass. *Seinfeld* would have died prematurely but for one senior executive at NBC who believed in it enough to fight for the funding to develop the next four episodes. The network gave the new installments a chance—and *Seinfeld* went on to win ten Emmy Awards and become, according to a *TV Guide* poll, the number-one TV series of all time.[1]

What does a TV sitcom have to do with branding? Plenty. Television programs are no less brands than are cars, soft drinks, and soap. *M*A*S*H*, *Friends, CSI, Law & Order,* and *American Idol* make a lot of money not only for the advertisers within the programs but for creators and producers who bring them to life.

Like any great brand, *Seinfeld* was successful because it was different. It wasn't built around a TV-family cliché. It didn't have a multigenerational cast. It was—famously—about nothing. *Seinfeld* simply made people laugh about ordinary life.

But because *Seinfeld* was so different, it took time to take root in people's minds. They didn't get it at first. The show was a rare breakthrough of creativity that was given the time it needed to develop. (*Seinfeld* didn't even crack the top 30 in the Nielsen ratings until its fourth season.)

Anything truly creative is, by definition, new. And new things are often different. Brands must be careful not to draw conclusions too soon after they launch a campaign. If they expect their branding to take off like a blockbuster movie, generating box office records on opening weekend, they are likely to be disappointed. Sure, some creative efforts break out immediately, but others take time to develop. And those that develop more slowly can have a great impact at a fraction of the cost.

It can take a while for a brand idea to sink in. People have to be exposed to the message over time, and they have to come to a point where their awareness of the product and trust in the brand align with their needs and natural purchase cycle. And that happens on their schedule, not yours.

> **The most meaningful storylines sometimes take the longest to develop.**

It helps if you think of each aspect of your branding efforts not as 30 seconds of airtime, a quarter page in a magazine, or a banner, tweet, or post but as an episode of a TV series. Each execution develops an element of your story in a continuing saga that builds identification and affection over time. If you change direction too rapidly, it won't reflect well on your brand. And it will get very, very expensive.

Some *Seinfeld* episodes were better than others. Some of your executions will be better than others—as measured by surveys, traffic, sales, or other short-term metrics. But if you've done your homework and believe in your brand, let it breathe a little. Let it grow up and find its voice. You'll be much more likely to build equity over time by making slow, deliberate improvements rather than herky-jerky changes.

Not even a hit series is a hit every night. Commit to unfolding the story of your brand over time, and don't ask any one element of your branding program to do too much. You still may hit on an occasional blockbuster, but you will also be more likely to develop a storyline that will keep people tuned in.

59
VISIBILITY BRINGS CREDIBILITY

IN THE INTRODUCTION, I TOLD THE STORY OF MY ENLIGHTENING (and embarrassing) television purchase experience. Normally, Circuit City would have been on my list as one of the stores in which to shop, but the struggles the company was then facing (soon to be followed by bankruptcy) made me nervous.

I was sure I could somehow get my TV serviced under the manufacturer's warranty if something were to go wrong, but I figured it would be more of a hassle if the retailer from which I purchased the TV wasn't there to back me up. So I went elsewhere.

This principle, which I call "the fear of warranty," is one of the reasons why GM did everything it could to avoid the normal bankruptcy process. We all feel less comfortable doing business with companies we perceive are on the ropes, and GM believed that fact alone would hasten its demise.

The company was probably correct in its analysis. I submit that a similar principle holds true at the other end of the spectrum as well. Brands that are setting the world on fire make people feel more confident about (and perhaps even more intelligent for) doing business with them. And one very visible signal a brand can send about its momentum is how consistently it's out there.

You probably have at least a vague familiarity with the names Michael Beschloss and Doris Kearns Goodwin. They're the presidential historians who always seem to be called on by the television networks to provide expert commentary during campaign seasons. They really seem to know their stuff.

Of course, you and I can't say with certainty whether they are the most qualified historians to comment on presidential elections. Oh, sure, they are intelligent, studied academics who provide interesting insights. But there are probably many other capable people who could do the same.

What makes us believe that Beschloss and Goodwin are the leading experts is the fact that they are consistently visible, presumably because they've been vetted by people who should know. The fact that we regularly see them on TV is, in and of itself, evidence of their expertise. Simply put, their visibility gives them credibility.

> **Don't underestimate the I've-seen-you factor.**

The same is true with brands we see that are active in the marketplace day after day. All other things being equal, the more visible a brand is, the more it builds trust with customers and prospects.

Consider some of today's most successful brands. Without personally spending a great deal of time and effort researching, testing, and comparing competitive alternatives, we don't really know whether Toshiba makes a better TV, Intel makes a faster processor, or Verizon has a better network. Instead, we entrust at least some of our judgment to the momentum these brands appear to have in the marketplace.

In some respects, it doesn't even matter what their ads say; the simple fact that each of these companies is actively and consistently "in the game" speaks volumes—especially in challenging economic times—and generates genuine momentum for their brands.

James Surowiecki, author of *The Wisdom of Crowds*, makes the case that "together all of us know more than any one of us does." He says, "Markets are made up of diverse people with different levels of information and intelligence, and yet when you put all those people together and they start buying and selling, they come up with generally intelligent decisions."[1]

In the world of branding, consistency is like a scorecard on the wisdom of crowds. People know that advertising is expensive, so the more a company is out there, the more successful it must be. And the more successful it is, the more it means that other people are choosing it. Which means that it may be a good idea for you and me to choose it as well.

Any brand can benefit from this power of positive momentum. Through its branding efforts, people will learn that it exists. With repeated exposure, they'll learn that it's stable. With even more repeated exposure, they'll assume it's successful—after all, based on its ability to sustain a long-term branding program, it must be.

The specific content of a brand's messaging is, of course, of vital importance as well—Beschloss and Goodwin wouldn't last long if they were misleading, annoying, or ignorant. But what's true of careers, of sports, and of life in general is also true of branding: Don't underestimate the power of simply showing up.

60

HARMONY IS HARD

THERE'S TREMENDOUS ADVANTAGE IN THE LEARNING THAT comes from eating, sleeping, and breathing one brand, in one industry, day in and day out. But there's also advantage in the cross-pollination of ideas that come from working with multiple brands in multiple industries over time. Partnerships that leverage the strengths of both can be powerful indeed. I'm talking about client–agency relationships.

Ask anybody who controls a branding budget and they'll tell you there's no shortage of agencies lining up to work with them. But finding the right match is critical, and it's easy to make a selection based on the wrong criteria. That causes heartache, inefficiency, and a significant amount of lost productivity.

If you're in the market for an agency, begin by noticing the branding efforts that you admire. Look for campaigns that you think are smart, or creative, or have been around for a long time (a good indicator of success), and find out who did them. Most of the time a simple search will turn up the name of the agency, or you can call the brand advertised and simply ask them who does their work. Another idea is to page through award annuals. Yes, awards matter. Research shows a high correlation between award-winning advertising and sales results. As with your hairstylist, your golf instructor, your cardiologist, or the captain who's piloting your plane, it only makes sense to hire someone whose peers have a great deal of respect for their work.

Don't screen out agencies based on size. Consider how small agencies develop: Talented people enter the business working for an established agency. The good ones grow with the agency. The great ones move up and eventually run the agency. And the really great ones think: "I can do this better myself" and go off to start their own shops. It's a continuous cycle of renewal, and talented people at the helm of small agencies are likely to have more experience than the midlevel staffers that would be assigned to your account at a big firm.

Also, don't make industry experience a requirement. What most brands need is to increase their differentiation from competitors, and agencies with a lot of category experience might be subject to industry groupthink. No agency will ever know as much as you do about your industry, so you should hire it for what it does know: the art of branding.

Pick a few agencies and initiate a conversation. Spend a few minutes on the phone with them, and you'll get an immediate sense of chemistry and interest. Ask about the history of the firm, their current clients, their internal culture and their principles. Ask if they've heard of your brand and are aware of its issues. If yes, explore their initial, top-of-mind thinking. If not, don't necessarily dismiss them. Not everybody can stay on top of every industry.

> **The more care you take in hiring an agency, the less often you'll have to do it.**

Then invite them to your place to review a handful of case studies. Keep in mind that you're not looking to see if they have good outcomes to report (all of them will) but to understand the thinking behind how they arrived at their solutions. Learn about their process: what it is, how it works, and how it might fit your company and culture. Is it methodical? Inspiration based? Involving? Inventive?

Imagine your brand at their agency and see how they would go about addressing your issues. Don't ask for—or even entertain—speculative work. The timeline is artificial, the discovery process is shortchanged, and in the excitement of a new business pitch, an agency can focus disproportionate resources on the task, something unlikely to happen in an ongoing relationship. Plus, the more an agency is willing to jump through speculative hoops for you, the more your suspicion should be raised. If an agency is ready to give away its work, there must not be a very good market for it.

Once you've narrowed your list to two or three firms, spend time at each shop. Meet their teams. Experience their culture. Initiate conversations with people in each department. Inquire about their jobs. Ask to see what they're working on (as long as it's not confidential). Go out to lunch with them. See if you like them, and give them the opportunity to do the same.

Have them answer a handful of difficult questions. Don't surprise them with the questions, but send them ahead of time. The point is to get honest insight, not quick comebacks. Just like in any relationship, you're probing to gain a sense of the agency's personality and character.

When you find a good fit, discuss with the agency the best way to ensure a long and successful relationship. Come to clear agreement on your expectations for staffing, compensation, and service. Then fire the starter's gun and let the agency get to work.

Forming a successful client–agency partnership is not a simple task. It takes time. But it's better to do it right once than wrong twice (or three or four times). A bad agency decision can set your brand back years. Go through the discipline and hard work of making a good choice. Then you can get down to the fun and excitement of inventing the future together.

WHOOPS

BRANDING IS AN IMPERFECT SCIENCE, AND EVEN THE BEST
brands slip up now and then. The more we can learn from their mistakes, the less likely we'll be to make them.

61
IT'S OK TO BE UNCOMFORTABLE

CLIENT–AGENCY RELATIONSHIPS CAN BE THE STUFF OF LEGEND. While a few are like the storybook marriage of Paul Newman and Joanne Woodward (who met in 1953 and spent the next 55 years together in wedded bliss), others resemble Elizabeth Taylor's and Richard Burton's tempestuous relationship or Kim Kardashian's 72-day marriage to NBA star Kris Humphries.

Such was the case with CareerBuilder and its agency, Cramer-Krasselt. CareerBuilder is the largest online job site in the United States, serving more than 24 million unique job seekers each month and nine out of ten Fortune 1,000 corporations. But the fast-growing Web site gave itself a public relations black eye and spent unnecessary resources by overreacting to unreliable research.

The brand had put itself on the map via a run of creative and attention-getting Super Bowl ads. The "I work with a bunch of monkeys" campaign increased CareerBuilder's annual revenues sevenfold and made it number one in market share. But shortly thereafter, Career-Builder fired the agency that created those ads.

Cramer-Krasselt's mistake? Taking a creative risk. Trying to top itself in a subsequent Super Bowl, the agency developed an evolution of the campaign that maintained its slapstick sense of humor but added some complexity and nuance (you can't get much less nuanced than monkeys).

Unfortunately, the new commercials didn't crack the top 10 in *USA Today*'s Ad Meter, a poll of a whopping 238 people conducted after the Super Bowl. The next thing the agency knew, CareerBuilder was inviting other firms to pitch. It was a sudden, and stunning, decision. As *Advertising Age*'s Bob Garfield put it, it was "like shutting down Butterball because someone in Indiana said the Thanksgiving turkey was dry."[1]

CareerBuilder did what many brands do at the first sign of distress: fire the agency. Week after week, *Adweek* and *Advertising Age* chronicle the tawdry business of client–agency breakups. Like car accidents that nobody wants to see yet everyone stares at, readers of the trades cringe at the carnage, knowing that next time the names in those headlines could be theirs.

The published reasons brands fire their agencies are notoriously clichéd. "Commercial objectives require a new approach to strongly position our brand and service offerings in a competitive marketplace." "We feel that in the spirit of continuous improvement that is part of everything we do, we had the responsibility to see how the market has changed since our last review cycle." "As a part of our normal course of business, we review agency relationships on a periodic basis to make sure we are best meeting our evolving business needs."

There are plenty of good reasons why a brand would give its advertising agency its walking papers—lying, cheating, and disloyalty, to name a few. And sometimes an agency just isn't performing. But how do you decide when its time is up? How do you distinguish between a rough patch (which all brands and agencies go through) and a ruined relationship? When do you make the decision to spend valuable time and money to transition to a new agency—time and money that are always more significant than you anticipate?

I believe there is one overriding question you can ask yourself that will provide great insight into what you should do: Has my agency stopped challenging me?

You'll note that I said "stopped" challenging, not "started."

I'm not suggesting that an agency should challenge your authority. It's your money and your brand, and no matter how strongly an agency feels about its own opinion, it should never forget that. But the fact that you've got precious resources on the line is precisely why an agency should consider challenging your thinking part of its job description. After all, creativity requires thinking differently. Thinking differently requires risk taking. And risk taking is challenging.

If your ad agency isn't regularly making you feel uncomfortable, it's not doing its job. It may come to you with smart creative executions that nevertheless make you nervous because you've never seen it done that way before. It may push you to experiment with unproven tactics so that you don't get left behind in the frenetic world of new media. It may challenge you to reexamine your strategic approach altogether. Whatever the nature of the challenge, an agency that makes you think is taking the initiative to think on its own. And that's what you're paying it to do.

> **An agency that isn't challenging you isn't doing its job.**

This doesn't mean that its ideas and opinions will always be right. But two heads are better than one, and an external perspective is always worth considering. Such an approach will help ensure that you don't become complacent and that your brand doesn't grow stagnant.

Of course, the difficult thing about being challenged is that it's, well, challenging. Sometimes you just want the agency to do what you say, give you something familiar, or avoid rocking the boat. But you wouldn't want your attorney or accountant to be an order taker, no matter how much she complicates your life. Once your agency loses its passion, you've lost a key strategic asset.

Think about the interactions you've had with your agency over the past year. Have you been challenged? Have you been pushed? Have you felt a little bit annoyed by the fact that the managers of your account always want you to go just one step beyond what you're comfortable with? If so, the relationship is probably worth saving, and you can focus on fixing any bumps in the road you may be experiencing.

If not, consider turning the tables and giving the agency a challenge. Share something you're struggling with, give it an assignment, or simply articulate a problem statement and tell the agency to break new ground—strategically, creatively, whatever. Then see how it responds.

If the agency surprises you, you've just rejuvenated the relationship and saved yourself the time and hassle of a review. But if it's lost the fire or simply doesn't come through, then you're paying too many bucks for too little bang—and the opportunity cost of not moving forward is losing you brand equity every day. If that's the case, it's time to move on.

62
ENTROPY HAPPENS

THERE'S A SAYING IN THE AGENCY WORLD THAT BRANDS GET THE advertising they deserve, regardless of how good the agency with which they partner is. Such is the case with Burger King, a company whose sales results sometimes seem as random as the behavior of the teenagers it targets. The brand's on-again, off-again success is interesting to watch from the outside but no doubt frustrating within.

Yes, McDonald's is a formidable rival. Yes, Subway has been killing it with its "fresh" focus for several years. Yes, newer brands like Panera and Chipotle all take their bites. But competition is a fact of life for every brand. Burger King's woes are largely of its own making.

After a several-year run of growth that rebuilt some confidence between the corporate office and its franchisee community, Burger King's then CEO, John Chidsey, ticked off his franchisees by appropriating funds from soft-drink makers that normally go to store owners.[1] It's not like he was doing anything untoward with the money—it was going to support the national advertising fund, which would drive even more business into the stores. But Burger King's independent-minded franchisees didn't like someone changing the rules, especially if it meant money was coming out of their pockets.

This minor rift may have been a problem in any company, but with Burger King it was more of a whopper (sorry, couldn't resist). Chidsey was soon after replaced by Bernado Hees, who himself was then replaced by Daniel Schwartz. Meanwhile, the company was acquired by 3G Capital in 2010 and then went public (for the second time) in 2012.[2] Not exactly the picture of stability.

What has ailed Burger King over the years isn't a lack of ideas from the parade of CEOs and ownership groups. The company simply couldn't sustain agreement on a clear direction.

Burger King consistently stumbles on one of the four internal dynamics that our research reveals commonly derail companies: a lack of internal alignment. In physics, this is known as entropy—the tendency of everything in the universe to trend toward disarray. You don't go through more than a dozen CEOs (and half as many agencies) over a 20-year period unless something is fundamentally wrong.

It's natural for companies that are struggling to try to pin the tail on external issues like competition, recession, or government regulation. And those issues do play a role. But research and experience alike demonstrate that the bigger challenge is ensuring that the management team—and in the case of a franchise company, the franchise community—are in alignment.

> **If you're not pulling together, you're pulling apart.**

My firm specializes in working with stalled, stuck, and stale brands, and we do a lot of research in that arena. One of our tools is a self-diagnosis where we ask management teams a penetrating series of questions to uncover what's really going on within their organizations. We recently pooled those statistics and found that nearly half of the struggling company professionals we surveyed have been derailed by a lack of alignment, and a full 59 percent admit they're struggling with internal discord.

How can any brand expect to make progress when its people are pulling in different directions? Turnover in the executive suite only exacerbates the problem, since every new CEO expects (and deserves) to be able to determine the direction in which he or she thinks the company should go. But what any enlightened CEO must understand is that internal alignment is at least as important as external strategy.

A college basketball coach might be able to come up with a dynamite game plan, but if the assistant coaches and players aren't on board, they won't put up a lot of points. And even the boosters should understand that a change in head coaches isn't always the answer; alignment comes in part from continuity.

If things aren't going right for your brand, by all means examine your strategy. But by no means stop there. Take a hard look within and be willing to recognize misalignment in your team. It doesn't mean that everybody must agree on everything, but they all must be on the same page in an atmosphere of mutual trust.

63
SIZE WON'T SAVE YOU

HOW CAN THE NATION'S SECOND LARGEST *ANYTHING* GO BANKrupt?

Even in the toughest of times, there should be room for at least two competitors. Smaller, weaker players tend to be the ones that run out of cash, customers, and time, while the biggest companies use the advantages that come with size to ride out the storm. At least that's how it normally works.

The most oft-cited reason for the demise of Circuit City, the original electronics and appliance superstore, was the economic tsunami that swamped the world beginning in late 2007. But it's not the only reason. Archrival Best Buy, while also suffering the ill effects of unprecedented market tectonics and contending with the challenges of consumers who use its stores as showrooms then buy elsewhere online, managed to avoid suffering the same fate. In fact, it was Best Buy that put most of the nails in Circuit City's coffin.

Dating all the way back to the 1990s, Best Buy caught Circuit City flatfooted and continued to steal market share over a period of years. The aggressive chain repeatedly outmaneuvered its once-larger competitor, changing industry dynamics by paying hourly wages instead of commission and building larger, better-stocked stores, among other things. Best Buy continued to innovate in response to a changing marketplace; Circuit City didn't.

Circuit City's former chairman and CEO, Alan Wurtzel, admitted as much, saying the chain wasn't able to change quickly enough once the recession dealt the fatal blow.[1] Not unlike Burger King's source of woes,

Wurtzel blames a lack of focus inside the company brought about in part by a succession of CEOs. Circuit City was also distracted by diversions, such as its venture into automotive retailing and its launch of an ill-fated digital videodisc system.

While Best Buy was sharpening its business model, Circuit City stubbornly clung to the commissioned-salesperson model. The company made a series of bad real estate decisions, failed to leverage the rise of video games, missed the early stages of the software explosion, and quit selling appliances. Almost inexplicably, Circuit City also failed to step up online just as e-commerce was beginning to take off. Management developed new plans but didn't stick with them long enough to see things through. That led to, according to Wurtzel, a "decision of the week or the month" mentality within the company.[2]

Then came a destructive internal culture clash brought about by the last CEO, Philip Schoonover, who infamously fired 3,400 of the brand's best employees and replaced them with cheaper staff.[3] That only added to the disillusionment of an already-discouraged employee base. Dealing with too much inventory after an ill-timed billion-dollar stock buyback, Circuit City didn't have the cash to survive the recession and filed for bankruptcy in 2008.

> **Don't rest on your laurels. What got you here won't get you there.**

Of his successors, Wurtzel says, "They underestimated the change in consumer taste, the change in consumer buying patterns and they clearly underestimated the rapid rise of Best Buy." Wurtzel even wrote a book about the brand's demise, *Good to Great to Gone: The 60 Year Rise and Fall of Circuit City.*

Power branding isn't just a catchphrase for how to win friends and influence people. Its principles are what are required to remain competitive in a continually changing environment. Best Buy's moves—and Circuit City's own internal dynamics—put the latter on the ropes well before it was hit by the economic crisis. Weak as it was, Circuit City simply couldn't withstand the blow.

64
YOU CAN'T FAKE AUTHENTICITY

IN THE MIDST OF THE GREAT RECESSION, A FULL-PAGE NEWSPA-
per ad from Citibank caught my eye. Considering the mess-of-its-own-
making from which the bank was suffering, the ad featured an unusual
headline: "Providing Stability. Securing the Future."

Clearly, I thought, someone in the marketing department is not
paying attention. Citi was not only being buffeted by the storm, it was
one of the causes of it. A company whose actions had led to so much
financial upheaval laying claim to stability seemed detached at best,
disingenuous at worst. (Ironically, the ad also featured the bank's long-
standing slogan—"Citi never sleeps," which, given the mess the company was in, I surmised was truer than ever.)

After years of telling us to "Live Richly" prior to the financial melt-
down, Citi began professing "responsible finance" as the new corner-
stone that would drive everything it does. Such a claim was a stretch, to
say the least, as it violated a key tenet of power branding: authenticity.

Consumers won't tolerate the disingenuousness of headline-making
mischief caused by companies such as Citi, Enron, Madoff, and BP. And
the advent of social media has given them more power than ever to expose pretenders. In such an environment, it behooves everyone in business to consider the extent of their brand's authenticity. Nobody wants
to be exposed as a fraud.

As in human relationships, if you try to be something you're not, it
won't ring true—and it won't be long until you get called on it. Celebrities may appear beautiful on *Entertainment Tonight,* but when they say
ugly things on answering machines, the world soon finds out. Athletes

who are heroes on the field but scoundrels in real life can get away with living double lives for only so long. Companies that lay claim to something they're not can be called on it with increasing speed and fervor.

In branding, it's not so much lying that's the problem (with a few notable exceptions), it's embellishing the truth—usually in the form of braggadocio. Claiming to have "the best service," "the best prices," or some other cliché won't fly unless it's truly, demonstrably, and consistently true. Every brand wants to be well regarded, but overpromising is a temptation to which too many brands surrender.

> **Just because you say it doesn't make it true.**

As we've seen, sometimes it pays to take the opposite tack by admitting a negative about your brand or category. Since a company is unlikely to confess to something that isn't true, doing so is an honest way to begin to build trust. Remember Joe Isuzu, the smile-while-you-lie car salesman? He became a pop culture icon based on the principle that if there's an element of truth to something, you might as well come clean about it.

Authenticity also requires credibility. I remember staying at a hotel that had paper-thin walls, which became evident when my neighbors, a rather energetic high school softball team, enjoyed too much fun and too little sleep (as did I). When I dragged my weary body into the bathroom the next morning, there on the shower curtain was the hotel brand's chirpy slogan: "Wake up on the bright side." Not a credible promise. (That said, I did have some sympathy for the parent company. Authenticity is a particularly vexing problem for franchised companies that leave the customer experience in the hands of independent operators, some of whom care less than others.)

Depending on your starting point, it may take time to earn the credibility that comes with consistency. Citi's intentions may be as authentic as they get, but given the company's history, it's going to be a while before most people believe any claims it makes.

Every brand can find its place of authenticity. If you're in business and you're making a profit, you're obviously doing something right for someone. Start there and discover exactly what it is you do that is ringing customers' bells. I once drove past a bail bonding company in a ramshackle building with a beat-up sign that said: "Because jail sucks." Now that's authentic—not to mention funny. I'm not in the market for a bail bond (and hope never to be), but if something bad happens this weekend, I know who to call.

Continually strive to make your brand the best it can be. Just never try to make it something other than what it is.

65
FREE IS COSTLY

FREE. SOME SAY IT'S THE MOST POWERFUL WORD IN THE English language. Others romance it as a magical marketing term. Using "free" to lure leery customers can be tempting indeed. But you might want to think twice about that.

Don't get me wrong. As a consumer, I like getting something for nothing. In commerce, however, there's really no such thing—anything of value costs somebody something. When companies make a gratis offer, what they're really doing is muddying the cost-benefit equation and making it more difficult for their prospects to make a clear value determination. It's kind of like getting a big tax refund; it feels like found money, but offering a no-interest loan to the government isn't to your advantage.

Still, there's no doubt that "free" can be irresistible to consumers, especially those who are adept at gaming the system without purchasing anything. (They sure aren't the ones you want to attract.) Few brands recognize the damaging effects that free offers can achieve, even when they do lure people to buy. You might call these effects the Three Ds.

Free is *dangerous*. Price isn't just a reflection of value; it's an indication of it. When something is offered free for any length of time, people begin to value it less. Over time, this makes them unwilling to pay a premium for it—or pay for it at all. It may seem at first as if "free" helps your value proposition, but ultimately it hurts it.

Remember when it felt really special to get a free basic cell phone when you signed a two-year service contract? Now we've come to expect it. Similarly, many newspapers are struggling with their online properties, trying to charge readers for content after having offered it free for years. Watch: As e-commerce companies increasingly offer free shipping and more hotels offer free high-speed Internet service, both will become ever more difficult to charge for. We'll still pay for them—via costs that are buried in other charges.

Free is *duplicable*. If you can offer something for free, so can your competitors. The more people pick up on your offer, the more quickly your competitors will match it. What might begin as a temporary tactical advantage can quickly become an industry albatross—can you say "frequent flyer program"?

A grocery chain near me began doubling the value of coupons people brought in from their Sunday-morning circulars. The move attracted a lot of attention, and competing chains soon matched the offer. Soon enough a coupon war was on, and it didn't end until triple- and even quadruple-coupon offers decimated the chains' razor-thin margins. They finally called it quits after losing millions of dollars. This story has been repeated thousands of times in hundreds of industries, from fast food to industrial equipment.

> **The more you give away, the more it will cost your brand.**

Free is *deceptive*. Not to your customers, although I could make a case for that. It's deceptive to you. It's easy to forget that there are four marketing Ps: If your product, place, and promotion don't add up to something of clear value, you can't expect pricing to bail you out. Car dealers have historically been the poster children of this approach, shouting and screaming about free giveaways and low prices when the bigger problem (and significant opportunity) is how awful the car-buying experience tends to be. It's as if they're blind to what ails them.

Other brands that advertise seasonally or otherwise infrequently can misunderstand the danger as well. Instead of steadily building brand equity around a real value proposition, they expect to measure the immediate impact of every ad. That makes it natural for them to turn to the "magic word," not realizing that such a short-term focus often compromises their long-term prospects. Offering something for nothing seems so easy, when in reality it can be one of the hardest things from which to recover.

As with discounting, "free" is fine in small doses for limited periods of time, such as a free initial consultation or a free sample of a new product at the supermarket. It's both smart and polite to offer something at no charge as a gesture of courtesy or appreciation to existing customers, from free parking to an occasional thank-you gift. Doing so can have a positive effect, precisely because it's after the sale: Customers have already accepted your price/value proposition as reasonable, and the value of what you're offering them doesn't call that into question.

It's when you offer something for nothing as an enticement to buy that the danger sets in. If you try to fool your prospects by making your pitch about what's "free," you'll also be fooling yourself. Instead, focus on demonstrating real value and how you can get prospects to part happily with their money. You—and they—will be better off.

66
DOING GOOD MIGHT HURT

IN 2010 PEPSI DEVOTED MUCH OF ITS MARKETING BUDGET TO THE "Refresh Project," an ambitious effort to give away $20 million to deserving organizations that offer "refreshing ideas that change the world." While company management was enamored by that effort, sales declined nearly 10 percent in the first nine months of the year, and Pepsi lost critical market share.

Pepsi said the Refresh Project was meant to reflect the "optimistic and fun" spirit of Pepsi-Cola and that "the whole notion of allowing consumers to have a voice is really the wave of the future." PepsiCo CEO Indra K. Nooyi said, "It's a matter of, 'What does this brand stand for in terms of doing something positive in the world.'"[1] Hmmm. Sounds to me like Pepsi had a guilty conscience and thought it would offer an odd form of charitable penance as an apology for dealing in sugar and caffeine.

To be fair, the Refresh Project made an impact. In its launch phase, it generated some 76 million votes for more than 12,000 submissions, and the effort was recognized by fully one-third of consumers.[2] Beyond that, Pepsi generated millions of dollars of publicity value from the program and made a real difference for a number of charitable organizations.

That's all good. But it begged the question of what business Pepsi is in, and it only deepened the mystery as to why the program didn't refresh Pepsi's sales and market share. Oddly enough, some reports suggested that many Refresh Project grants went to organizations and individuals who aren't soda drinkers (and may even be anti-soda).[3] Sounds like a classic case of hitting the wrong target. After a dismal sales year, Pepsi began reinvesting in more traditional branding, stepping up its investment in measured media by double digits, and saw sales begin to recover.

Every company has limited resources with which to pursue its mission. It's possible for corporate social responsibility initiatives to lead to the unintentional neglect of the responsibilities to which company leaders should be most committed: advancing the interests of the organization. While nobody is for world hunger or against family farms, even such popular issues can become a distraction. As a general rule, the less directly an issue is linked to a company's core expertise and interests, the less willing the company should be to take it on.

TOMS Shoes was founded on the social mission of matching every pair of shoes purchased with a pair of new shoes for a child in need. In TOMS's case, the social mission is the same as the company mission. Similarly, Newman's Own was founded on the principle of donating all profits to charity (and it has done so, to the tune of $370 million and counting). These are companies whose corporate social responsibility programs are inseparable from their missions, and they pursue them appropriately. That wasn't the case with Pepsi.

Good intentions don't justify bad strategy.

Before you consider investing brand resources in a social initiative, remember that your primary responsibility is to act on behalf of your stakeholders. Don't confuse meeting their objectives with the need for some other form of social responsibility. As long as a brand behaves responsibly, making a profit—creating jobs, increasing wealth, and enhancing the health of the economy—is the most socially responsible thing it can do. Staying focused will also help ensure that your efforts to build awareness of what your brand is about and why it helps society aren't dismissed as manipulative or pandering.

Differing audiences (or interest groups) will judge the choices you make based on their differing perspectives. Your task is to sort through the issues and determine the best course of action for your brand. That's where it can get dicey if you don't keep first things first.

67

TACTICS ARE DECEIVING

IN 2004, OPRAH WINFREY MADE A BIG SPLASH WHEN SHE GAVE away a new car to nearly 300 deliriously happy audience members. The giveaway was yet another feather in Oprah's cap and proved to be a brilliant brand builder for her. But do you recall the car company that was behind it?

If you said Pontiac, congratulations. Although you're most certainly in the minority, the monster publicity the stunt received at the time may indeed have justified the brand's investment. Still, it didn't do much to build the long-term value of the now-defunct Pontiac brand. It was a classic case of a tactic in search of a strategy for a brand that had lost its focus.

Back in the 1960s and 1970s, Pontiac was defined by drool-inducing muscle cars such as the GTO, Firebird, and TransAm. The Pontiac brand meant power, styling, and cool. Its appeal wasn't for everyone, but it was powerful for some. But then Pontiac began introducing a host of new models like the Trans Sport (a minivan), Sunfire (a compact car), Aztek (an SUV crossover), and Vibe (a hatchback). It was unclear who, exactly, Pontiac was *not* trying to serve, which is another way of saying it was aiming to please too many masters. That's why the Oprah giveaway could be justified; given Pontiac's loss of focus, almost anything could have been.

Sometimes an idea appears so cool or daring that it just cries out to be implemented. Sometimes a brand wants to be on the cutting edge or jump into new waters. Sometimes you just want to make noise for your brand. In all of these cases, the temptation to rationalize can be powerful. But if the tactic doesn't enable you to make a relevant point to a strategic audience, it won't do you much good.

No brand is immune to this temptation. In 2002, Vodafone, the London-based telecommunications giant, sponsored two streakers who interrupted a rugby match in Sydney. Did the stunt get a lot of attention? You bet. (It also brought a big fine and a great deal of negative publicity.) Did it build the Vodafone brand? I'm not sure how.

Quiznos became infamous for a short time a few years back when it introduced a series of TV commercials starring singing "Spongmonkeys." The spots were certainly attention getting, but the association of what appeared to be rodents and sub sandwiches is not what I would call smart strategy. One local newspaper in Denver, where Quiznos is based, cited a store manager who said her business dropped 20 to 30 percent while the spots were airing. She said one woman even stopped her in a store and told her the ads made her grandchildren cry.[1]

Beware any tactic that's in search of a strategy.

Why did Quiznos hitch its brand to the Spongmonkeys' wagon? Apparently the commercials tested well in focus groups—methodology was their first mistake. But the idea originated out of a cult following that a London artist had developed for his cute little creatures. Somebody fell in love with this "tactic" and force-fit it to Quiznos. One person on YouTube summed it up best: "As much as I love this commercial (which I do . . . it's hilarious!), I don't ever want to eat at Quiznos. Eew."[2]

Branding isn't just about creating impressions or getting attention. To be truly effective, the visibility your brand generates should be relevant to its strategy. When you're faced with a new tactical opportunity, no matter how exciting it appears, run it through the filter of your brand idea. If it's consistent, it may be a good opportunity to generate additional exposure. If not, you can find better uses for your money.

Generating attention is one thing. Generating relevant attention is what really matters. Put strategy first, and make sure every tactic you pursue serves the bigger picture.

68
PRICE IS A PRODUCT FEATURE

THE CHIEF EXECUTIVE OF NOW-DEFUNCT ULTIMATE ELECTRONICS long served as the brand's spokesperson, and in his advertising he insisted Ultimate always had the lowest prices. He boasted that his company continuously shopped the competition, and when Best Buy or another competitor lowered the price on something, Ultimate Electronics lowered it even further.

Whether or not most consumers believed this was beside the point (I suspect they didn't—we've all learned that lowest-price promises are often empty). What I can't figure out is how Ultimate Electronics expected to build long-term success with this strategy. The chain tended to attract price-driven shoppers who were likely to have zero brand loyalty. That might have sold a razor-thin-margin TV today, but it didn't build equity for tomorrow. Even in the cutthroat world of consumer electronics, low prices are not always your friend.

Say you were in a store like Ultimate Electronics evaluating two home entertainment systems that had similar features and design characteristics but were significantly different in price. Which would you choose? Many people would choose the lower-priced option, but some would go with the more expensive model. Would the latter group be acting irrationally? Not at all—even those who went with the cheaper option would most likely agree the more expensive one is somehow of higher quality. It would have to be (goes the reasoning) to justify its higher price.

Higher prices may lead to lower transaction volume in the short term, but they also provide the margins companies need to invest in brand building or to expand their distribution networks. Sending a quality signal via higher pricing is an undervalued, and often overlooked, strategy.

I once saw a poster in a convenience store trumpeting the virtues of its affordable, freshly brewed coffee. The headline said, "Because your morning coffee shouldn't cost more than your lunch." The obvious dig at Starbucks made me chuckle.

But it also made me think. Why shouldn't it? Is paying $3, $4, or even $5 for a cup of coffee really so irrational? Perhaps so if all you're buying is coffee, but if along with it you enjoy a relaxing, pleasant experience, it may be quite a bargain. In today's fast-paced culture, how much is ten minutes of bliss worth?

That thought reminded me of another shopping experience, this time revolving around jewelry. I inherited a ring from my grandmother that was somewhat dated but featured a beautiful aquamarine, my wife's birthstone. I knew she would love the stone, so I set out to find a jeweler who could redesign the ring into a pendant in time for her birthday.

> **Raising your price may enhance your appeal.**

I visited three or four different jewelry stores, trying to find one that would offer design talent, a personal touch, and a willingness to work within my budget. And as I evaluated my own decision process, I observed something interesting and somewhat surprising—I gravitated toward the most expensive option.

I can't say that the jeweler I chose was definitively better than the others, but for some reason I felt more comfortable with it, not in spite of its higher prices but *because* of them. I felt that by paying a little extra, I would be more assured of ending up with a piece my wife would love.

These are good examples of how price is a product feature, regardless of whether it's intended to be. For all I know, Starbucks might use the same coffee beans as the convenience store, but its higher price suggests a more valuable blend. The gold and diamonds my chosen jeweler sells may be identical to those found at other stores, but the fact it charges a little more gives me the sense that the quality of its work is better. And Ultimate Electronics might have provided just as good a shopping experience or warranty as its higher-priced competitors, but if it truly had the lowest prices, it stands to reason that something else had to suffer.

These are rational conclusions for me to draw because thousands of previous purchase decisions have taught me that price isn't merely a reflection of product quality, it's an indicator of it as well. If something is more expensive, it's usually for good reason.

It can be odd to feel good about losing customers because your prices are too high, but if you're not, you may be backing yourself into a low-margin corner. And don't kid yourself—other than Walmart, very few companies can truly sustain a low-price positioning.

Remember, customers will ask for lower prices, but they don't always want them. Sometimes knowing they paid a bit more for something reinforces their choice and makes them feel better—about the purchase and about your brand.

69

FOCUS CAN BE FLEETING

SPEAKING OF WALMART, THE BRAND IS A STUDY IN CONTRASTS. Its low prices are awesome; its shopping experience, not so much. Its positioning is terrific, but its advertising leaves something to be desired. It has a rock-solid heritage in founder Sam Walton, but too often it loses sight of what makes its own brand special.

A few years ago the company announced it was cutting prices on some 10,000 items. With any other retailer that would be cause for celebration, but with Walmart it was a bit mystifying.

Walmart = Low Prices. Period. Not margins. Not promotions. Not rollbacks. If prices are always as low as possible—a fact of which Walmart has worked so hard for so long to convince us—how then could they be cut, especially across such a wide swath of products? In one of its "rollback" TV commercials, "Mike the truck driver" said, "Just by driving smarter routes and making sure our trailers are packed fuller, we save millions of dollars on fuel costs." Did the world's leanest company expect its customers to believe that it just figured that one out?

Judging from what Walmart chief marketing officer Stephen Quinn said of the decision to cut prices, it appears so: "We felt we needed to increase the intensity and excitement with our customer, especially the feeling that Walmart has great deals."[1]

"Great deals" are what you'd expect from J.C. Penney or Macy's, not Walmart. For decades, Walmart conditioned us to expect the "great deals" to be baked into its everyday low prices, not used as underpinnings of a grand promotion.

Instead of fiddling with margins and flirting with upscale customers, Walmart should never veer from touting its all-the-time, everyday, low-low-lowest prices. *Always*. It's the one company with the credibility to do so, and price promotions threaten that very credibility. Walmart needs its customers to believe that it always—always—gives them the lowest prices it can.

Losing focus is so easy to do in branding. Most of the people surrounding a branding effort are intelligent and creative, which means they can easily get bored and want to change direction. But while it's okay to explore a variety of different ways of executing on a brand idea, the brand idea itself should rarely, if ever, change. And in the normal course of business, change should be evolutionary, not revolutionary.

Walmart's woes came about in part because it wanted to widen its appeal to a broader range of people—those with higher incomes than the company's core customer base. But attempting to broaden its appeal was a mistake, as the results of my firm's study of hundreds of America's fastest-growing companies would have predicted.

> **Lose your focus and you're likely to lose your footing.**

The study compared companies that had lost their footing to those that managed to maintain or even increase growth over a two-decade period. It pinpointed characteristics that cause growth to stall, one of which was a loss of focus. In fact, brands that had stumbled were five times more likely to admit they'd lost focus. And they were more likely to believe that the marketplace had changed and they no longer knew their place in it.

Company after company makes the same mistake, believing that its brand equity can be stretched beyond its capabilities. It happens to the best of businesses in every industry.

In 2002, Volkswagen introduced the Phaeton, a luxury car more expensive than some of its upscale Audi models. Who wants to spend more than $60,000 for a VW? Not very many people, it turned out, which is why the Phaeton's sales never got off the ground in the United States.

Remember Boston Chicken? Once the darling of growth companies, Boston Chicken became Boston Market, losing its focus and stumbling badly. And superstar office supply retailer Staples lost focus several years ago, trying to broaden its appeal to the home-office user. In doing so, it became less of a good fit for its core customer—small businesses. (Once Staples realized this, it returned to its roots and began doing better.)

The next time someone suggests broadening your brand's appeal to a wider spectrum of customers, remind them of the advice given by one of the CEOs we interviewed for our study: "Be very, very relevant to your market. Be clear on your core and what your place in the value chain is." If Walmart can lose its focus, any company can.

70
ASPIRATIONS MAY BACKFIRE

YEARS AGO, I WAS WAITING IN LINE AT A NORWEST BANK BRANCH, bored. I started looking around and noticed a nearby counter card. It said: "Our mission is to exceed our customers' expectations." I couldn't help but smile because the brand had indeed exceeded my expectations—I had expected to wait in line for five minutes, and it had already taken ten.

Somehow I don't think that was the effect the bank was looking for. But that's the risk any brand takes when it advertises its aspirations. Norwest has since merged with Wells Fargo, but the promise remains a key component of its corporate values statement.[1] At least the bank is no longer promoting it—for now (grand promises have a way of making their way into ad campaigns).

There's nothing wrong with having aspirations. Aiming to exceed customer expectations is a lofty goal. But it's a goal that should be kept among internal audiences. Making the aspiration a headline or slogan only creates expectations that are impossible to achieve. Companies that make this mistake are simply setting their customers up for disappointment.

For years, Delta Airlines got away with a catchy little jingle saying, "We love to fly, and it shows." But it didn't always show, and eventually Delta's boast caught up with it. Once the airline went out on the limb of overpromise it was fair game, and TV funnyman David Letterman didn't hold back when he called Delta "Amtrak with wings."

Sometimes companies promote their aspirations because they can't boast about their accomplishments. Why would Ford say "Quality Is Job

One" unless it had been having a problem with quality? Advertising this aspiration simply alerts people to a reason not to buy a Ford. It's like a doctor saying, "Keeping my patients alive is job one." Not exactly confidence inspiring. Or take the slogan that flopped for United Airlines: "Rising." Rising from what? Bankruptcy?

The biggest offenders in this game may be brands that have monopolistic characteristics, like power and telephone utilities. Because they're not subject to the same market pressures as companies that face significant competition, they can become lazy and insular. As a result, their branding tends toward clichéd, lofty-sounding promises. Consumers, already frustrated by being forced to do business with these brands, are primed to put them through the wringer when they don't come through.

Take, for example, CenturyLink, one of the 800-pound telecommunications gorillas. Because of its sheer size, CenturyLink is able to spend a lot of money in branding. Some years ago the company (then known as Qwest) introduced a campaign featuring a slogan highlighting its "Spirit of service in action." As a customer who had recently suffered a bad experience with the company (and not the first), I could have sworn the slogan was "Spirit of service inaction."

Don't say it. Do it.

No brand is immune. I purchased a fountain drink at a convenience store that featured a pithy slogan on the cup: "We always treat you like royalty." I'm sure the people who came up with that line had the best of intentions, but the clerks charged with carrying it out didn't get the message. The unkempt counter and sticky floor made that clear.

Whether your brand enjoys the market dominance of a power or telephone utility or is just a small corner store, the principle remains the same. Take a good hard look at what you're promising customers. If it isn't something you're genuinely delivering day in and day out, quit promising it. Today's marketplace is too unforgiving for you to promise something you can't deliver.

71

CELEBRITIES BITE

TIGER WOODS IS ONE OF THE GREATEST ATHLETES OF ALL TIME. He was also the first athlete to earn $1 billion in product endorsements.[1] That is, until Thanksgiving weekend a few years back when his true stripes were revealed.

Nike, Titleist, Gatorade, Gillette, American Express, AT&T, EA Sports, Golf Digest, NetJets, Tag Heuer, TLC Laser Eye Centers, and Upper Deck, among others, all had to determine what to do with that information. Accenture, the global consulting firm that had perhaps linked its brand most visibly to Tiger, was the first major sponsor to cut ties with him.

For six years, Accenture aligned its brand with the golfer via its "Go on, be a Tiger" campaign that was meant to personify the company's integrity and high performance. Needless to say, Tiger Woods no longer embodied those words. The power of brand accretion that had been working for Accenture all those years suddenly backfired.

Tiger may have been the endorsement champ, but he's never been alone. Michael Jordan (Nike, Gatorade, Hanes, McDonald's, Chevrolet), Bill Cosby (Jell-O, Del Monte, Ford, Kodak), and Peyton Manning (Sony, MasterCard, DirecTV, Gatorade) have all been at the top of the heap of celebrity endorsers. And there are hundreds of other examples of famous endorsement deals, from Karl Malden for American Express, to Brooke Shields for Calvin Klein, to William Shatner for Priceline.

As Tiger Woods proved, celebrity endorsers aren't only pricey, they're risky. Because celebrities exist in the spotlight, surrounded by paparazzi eager to turn a stolen moment into a quick buck, the risk of getting caught doing something embarrassing is much higher than for the average Joe. Who would have thought Tiger Woods—perhaps the most disciplined athlete of all time—would have an alter ego?

And they don't even have to be alive to do it. You would think that Ben Franklin is a safe bet as the face of Franklin Templeton Investments. Yet anybody who has read David McCullough's bestselling biography of John Adams might disagree. McCullough paints a picture of Franklin that is less than flattering, and since reading the book, I've been given pause each time I see a Franklin Templeton ad. Once you tie your brand identity to a celebrity (living or dead), you're hostage to that person's image.

> **The equity you borrow is not your own. The trouble it may cause is.**

"Borrowed equity" is the term used to describe the value of a celebrity spokesperson. The premise is if Endorser A wears Product B and drinks Product C, maybe consumers will want to as well. But borrowed equity is just that—borrowed. It may rub off on the brand endorsed, but in the long run it belongs to the celebrity.

In some cases the match between person and product is strategic, such as Jordan's natural tie to Nike or Cosby's comical personality for a fun product like Jell-O. That's also the case for Wilfred Brimley's grandfatherly tone for healthy Quaker Oats and Dennis Haysbert's powerful frame and authoritative voice for the "Good Hands People" at Allstate. Sometimes the brand can be shown to demonstrably solve a celebrity's problem, such as Dan Marino and Mike Golic shedding unwanted pounds using NutriSystem.

In the 1970s, the Pittsburgh Steelers "Steel Curtain" defense was anchored by a hulk of a man nicknamed "Mean Joe" Greene. As it turned out, Greene wasn't so mean in real life, but when he roamed the gridiron, he struck fear in the hearts of opposing teams. That's why Coca-Cola's idea of having Mean Joe toss his jersey to a young boy in exchange for a bottle of Coke was brilliant. The commercial made charming use of Mean Joe's image, and Coke was the star.

But Catherine Zeta Jones for T-Mobile? Emmitt Smith for Just For Men? Jason Alexander for KFC? I suspect each of these companies could have trotted out research and Q-scores that justified their investments, but they spent a lot of money for the borrowed equity of a talking head. It may be flattering for corporate leaders to rub elbows with celebrities, but unless there is a natural strategic tie, it's not much more than an expensive date.

The surest way to ensure long-term value from a celebrity spokesperson is to invent one. Advertising agency giant Leo Burnett pioneered this approach with Tony the Tiger, the Jolly Green Giant, and the Pillsbury Doughboy. Budweiser made hay with frogs and a lizard a few years back, and the roly-poly Michelin Man recently made a comeback (slimmed down for a more health-conscious culture).

If you believe your brand is in need of additional equity, instead of borrowing it from a celebrity, develop it yourself. You may need to refocus your efforts on making your offering more appealing, more affordable, or more easily available (and perhaps all of the above). Or you may simply need to find a way to develop a more attention-getting, interesting, and compelling appeal.

Take the money you would otherwise hand over to an already well-paid celebrity and invest it in developing original creative ideas that will make your brand stand out. That way, the equity you build will be nothing but your own.

72

NOBODY LIKES A BULLY

LIFE IS NOT A ZERO-SUM GAME. OK, MAYBE IN POLITICS IT IS. IF your candidate wins, the other guy loses. That's one reason why political advertising tends to get increasingly malevolent as campaigns approach their climax.

In commerce, however, it's possible for competing brands to all win. Innovation and advances in productivity actually enlarge the pie, making it unnecessary for competitors to fight over the same slice. Or chicken wing, as it were.

Grilled chicken chain El Pollo Asado once got a little big for its britches and created an ad campaign (ostensibly making fun of KFC) that showed over-the-top clerks asking customers if they want "greasy or extra-greasy" chicken, wiping their oily hands up and down filthy aprons as they handed striped buckets across the counter. The campaign was funny and effectively demonstrated El Pollo Asado's point of difference. It also awakened a sleeping giant.

KFC responded to its much-smaller competitor with stepped-up advertising, price promotion, and threat of legal action that could have paralyzed El Pollo Asado. Shortly thereafter, El Pollo Asado discontinued its campaign, calling it ineffective. Whether the brand felt like it made its point or chickened out (pun intended), El Pollo Asado blinked.

As the great chicken caper demonstrates, following the politicians down the poisonous path, trying to build yourself up by taking your competition down, is a dangerous game.

True, Pepsi employed the strategy with great success with the Pepsi Challenge. Beginning in the mid-1970s, Pepsi conducted consumer taste tests that demonstrated more people prefer its taste to that of

Coke. Seizing the opportunity, Pepsi launched an aggressive ad campaign that won the brand market share and put Coca-Cola on its heels. The Pepsi Challenge has even been credited with Coke's ultimate decision to reformulate its recipe and launch New Coke, one of the biggest brand blunders of all time.

One of the reasons the Pepsi Challenge worked was because Pepsi was number two to Coke, and everyone knew it. Rather than being seen as bullying, this was perceived as the opposite—as David taking on Goliath, the little guy standing up for himself. It didn't hurt that the brand's core audience was "The Pepsi Generation"—a younger demographic that almost reflexively questioned the wisdom of its elders (this was the era of Vietnam and Watergate, after all). Plus, Pepsi was big enough that Coke was unable to crush it with media spending in response, which it easily could have done to a smaller brand. The Pepsi Challenge was the right idea at the right time based on the right set of circumstances. Not easy to repeat.

> **Don't try to build up your brand by tearing another down.**

When it comes to competitive and comparative advertising, there are a couple of easy rules. First, if you're bigger/badder/more successful than the other brand, never mention its name. Why use your valuable branding resources to build awareness of your competition, regardless of what you're saying about them? Plus, when a big guy picks on a little guy it looks like bullying, and consumers have a reflexive dislike of bullies.

Second, if you're the little guy, be careful about picking a fight with the big kid on the block. Sure, you may gain the sympathy and even admiration of onlookers for standing up for yourself, but you also might get pounded.

If you're considering taking on a competitor, stop and think about it. Consider other ways of accomplishing your goals. You never want to be the bully, and there are a variety of ways to beat a bully other than by taking him on directly. If you can't outmuscle him, perhaps you can outrun him. Or outsmart him. You'll not only end up with all your teeth, you'll have the satisfaction of beating him on your terms, not his.

73
CHRISTMAS ISN'T UNCOOL

WHEN I WAS A KID GROWING UP, THERE WAS ONE COMMERCIAL that used to come on every Christmas season that I really looked forward to. It was from Norelco, and it featured an animated Santa flying in a Norelco electric razor rather than his sleigh. Norelco even had some fun with its moniker, calling itself "Noelco" during the holidays with a tagline saying "Even our name says Merry Christmas." To this day I associate positive feelings with the brand.

There are other warm advertising traditions associated with Christmas, from the Budweiser Clydesdales to the Coca-Cola Santa. In fact, Coca-Cola invented the modern image of Santa Claus some 80 years ago, a fact of which, to its credit, it still proudly boasts.

But things have been changing of late. Take the TV commercial for Lowe's home improvement stores in which a clumsy young guy approaches a female warehouse employee and blurts out, "Would you be my wife?" Startled, the clerk hesitantly begins walking the man through the store until she realizes that all he wants is a woman's opinion about the gift he is thinking about buying for the love of his life.

But here's where the spot goes south: As the young man role-plays with the clerk, turning around and presenting the gift (presumably on Christmas morning), he looks at her and exclaims, "Happy Holidays!"

Happy holidays? Is that really what a husband would say to his wife? By trying to cover all the bases, the spot ended up feeling forced. It was a departure from reality and a prime example of the unreasonable fear brands have of saying the word "Christmas."

It used to be that people wrung their hands about the overcommercialization of Christmas. These days we have almost the opposite problem—Christmas in advertising is becoming anathema. Brands still want the huge spike in sales that the holiday provides, but they're afraid to acknowledge the holiday itself. That's illogical, at best.

It's amusing to watch brands trip over themselves trying to find politically correct substitutions as they avoid saying the dreaded "C" word. But "happy holidays" and "season's greetings" only go so far. They sound hollow and synthetic, and that kind of approach is no way to build a connection with your target audience.

It seems many brands have become so afraid of offending some mythical person out there that they're unwilling to express their true sentiments. After nearly 30 years in the branding business there's one thing I've learned: Every ad is offensive to someone. Still, I find it a stretch to think that wishing your customers a "Merry Christmas" is going to set somebody off. And if it does, well, there's a word for them: Scrooge.

> **Celebration and equivocation are strange bedfellows.**

Ah, you say, but Christmas is a religious holiday—what about people from other faiths? It's true that to millions of people, Christmas is the most religious holiday of the year, but to millions of others, it's all about Santa Claus and reindeer and stockings hung by the chimney with care. As the famous refrain goes, it truly is "the most wonderful time of the year," even for many who don't celebrate it as a religious holiday. And there's no reason why the recognition of one holiday precludes the celebration of others. Lumping them together only makes each less special.

Remember *A Charlie Brown Christmas?* It's perhaps the most popular Christmas television program of all time. For some 50 years this charming (and overtly religious) special has been delighting children of all ages, and it has lost none of its appeal. Why? Because people love Christmas.

If you want to take advantage of a potential spike in sales during the Christmas season, embrace the holiday. There's nothing that says you can't celebrate Hanukkah as well (and any other holiday, for that matter), and the same principles apply. It makes your brand appear both happy and polite, and that will accrue to your benefit.

By all means don't be insincere. If you don't want people to have a merry Christmas, don't say so. But if you do, don't be afraid to let your brand spread a little Christmas cheer. Otherwise, before long we'll all be reduced to humming holiday carols as we open our holiday cards and put holiday presents under our holiday trees. Not to mention dreaming of a white holiday.

To that, I say humbug.

74

SPEED CAN KILL

J. C. PENNEY HAS THE UNFORTUNATE HONOR OF COMPETING IN the brutal department store industry. Squeezed by low-priced general merchandise stores like Walmart and Target on one end and higher-end stores like Nordstrom and (by comparison) Macy's on the other, J. C. Penney (like its old nemesis, Sears) found itself increasingly getting squeezed.

Retail industry veteran and CEO Myron Ullman had done good work upgrading Penney's apparel, consummating deals with brands like Sephora and Liz Claiborne that would lend a positive halo effect to the brand and finding other ways to eke out a profit. Still, sales had declined for three straight years prior to 2010, and when Ullman retired in 2011, Penney's business was still driven by discounting.[1] The vast majority of its sales were below full price.

Enter Ron Johnson, the man with a Target brand pedigree who Steve Jobs brought on at Apple to lead that brand's foray into retail, which he did with incredible success. Johnson's plan was to eliminate coupons, reduce Penney's reliance on discounting, and turn the store into a place where hip brands sold exclusive merchandise. He was going to make JCP (his preferred moniker) cool again. One analyst commented on Johnson's hiring as "injecting rocket fuel into Mike Ullman's growth strategies of turning J. C. Penney into a more exciting brand."[2]

An apt metaphor "rocket fuel" turned out to be. The problem was that J. C. Penney was anything but a rocket. It was more like an old jalopy, and jalopies don't run on rocket fuel.

Neither the company nor its customers was ready for the sweeping change Johnson initiated, and the new CEO did himself no favors by commuting to his job in Plano, Texas, from his home in California. Regardless of the reasons why, it didn't look good to the employees whose beliefs were being challenged, ways of doing things were being disrupted, and in some cases lives were being upended—people Johnson was counting on to carry out his vision.

Sales fell by 25 percent in 2012, and same-store sales fell an additional 16.6 percent in the first quarter of 2013. That was too much for the J. C. Penney board, and shortly thereafter Johnson was ousted.[3]

Was Ron Johnson's strategic revamp of a tired yet iconic brand the right thing to do? Would it have worked? We'll never know. Certainly he had a proven track record. And his plan made sense based on all of the principles of power branding. But he moved too quickly, both for JCP's management and staff and for its evolving customer base. You might say that Johnson ran off Penney's old customer base more quickly than he could recruit a new one.

> **Pedal too far ahead and your team may give up the chase.**

I'm not pointing fingers. As a public company, J. C. Penney is subject to all the perverse expectations brought about by managing to meet quarterly numbers. Had Johnson slowed the changes down to a pace customers and employees could tolerate, the sales decline may have been less precipitous but more prolonged. He may have been out of a job either way.

Still, there's a good lesson for any brand for which change is the watchword: Be careful of your pace. When a new brand direction is on the drawing board, it's natural for those in the know to want to implement it immediately. But your two critical "whos"—your internal and external target audiences—may need time to adjust.

75

THE MIRROR CAN'T
BE TRUSTED

ONCE RON JOHNSON WAS OUT OF THE PICTURE AT J. C. PENNEY, the company re-hired Myron Ullman, the CEO who had retired less than two years earlier. Fears of continued decline, a cash crunch caused by operating in the red for so long, and the blood in the water that competitors like Macy's and Kohl's smelled (leading them to step up their own discounting) led Penney's to return to its old ways immediately.

Newspaper ads, aggressive couponing, and a Mother's Day "doorbuster" sale (offering discounts of as much as 40 percent) generated an uptick in sales and traffic as circular-seeking customers found their way back to the J. C. Penney they knew and loved.

Beyond the discounts, however, Penney also went big with a television campaign apologizing for the 17-month diversion. Set to clichéd images of moms and kids smiling and laughing as they go about life in their J. C. Penney clothes, a saccharine announcer intoned, "It's no secret; recently J. C. Penney changed. Some changes you liked and some you didn't, but what matters from mistakes is what we learn. We learned a very simple thing: to listen to you. To hear what you need. To make your life more beautiful. Come back to J. C. Penney; we heard you. Now we'd love to see you."

It was a classic case of marketing to the mirror. Just as your thumb appears immense when held up close to your face, the brass at J. C. Penney couldn't see past the mess they had to clean up. It would be natural for them to think that all eyes were on them, watching and waiting to see what they would do. While that was certainly true of employees, shareholders, and certain sectors of the investment community, they didn't have to broadcast their mea culpa to 300 million Americans, most of whom didn't know and couldn't care less what was going on behind the scenes at the company. And for J. C. Penney's forlorn former customers, the circulars and coupons were enough to bring them back.

Marketing to the mirror manifests itself in a variety of different ways. It's easy to project your own thoughts, opinions, attitudes, and behaviors onto your customers and prospects. But while you might share some things in common with them, there will always be fundamental differences.

Here are five common ways the marketing-to-the-mirror mistake can manifest itself. See how many have tripped you up.

1. *The giant logo.* Not only do you love your brand, you're paying for the space or time and, by gosh, you want to see a big, bright logo beaming from it. Your prospective customers, however, are either unfamiliar with your brand or have some incomplete or mistaken impression of its value to them. If they're accosted by a giant logo before your marketing message has had a chance to get through, they may skip the ad and miss the point entirely.

> It doesn't matter what you think. What matters is what they think.

2. *The overstuffed ad.* Have you ever heard a radio commercial in which the words went by so fast that you couldn't process anything? Seen an ad in a magazine so riddled with bullet points that you don't know where to begin? Or driven past a billboard loaded with so much copy that it would take binoculars and three changes of the traffic light to process? In branding, as in many things in life, less is often more. Additional words do not always translate to better communication. On the contrary, they're likely to hinder it.

3. *The magic slogan.* Ah, the slogan: so misunderstood, so overappreciated. You and your team put so much time and effort into

creating those three or five little words that they're overflowing in meaning and packed with power—to you. To the rest of the world, they're just three or five little words. As we've seen, they may make a nice ribbon to tie around your advertising package, but they're not the package itself—and certainly not the prize inside.

4. *The "my" buy.* Who listens to jazz radio? Or classical music? Or that easy listening station that drones on in dentist offices and elevators? I don't. But a lot of people do. If they didn't, those formats wouldn't exist. We all gravitate naturally to the radio stations we listen to, the TV programs we watch, the Web sites we visit, the newspapers and magazines we read, and the social networks in which we participate. There's nothing wrong with advertising in places you personally frequent, as long as they're good outlets to reach people you're targeting. Just don't make the mistake of thinking that because something is of interest to you, it's of interest to them—or that because it's irrelevant to you, it's irrelevant to them.

5. *The one-hit wonder.* It's likely that you find your ads quite convincing: One exposure and you're sold. Alas, that's not the way things work in the cluttered and cacophonous world of modern communications. If you're wondering why your new advertising isn't setting the world on fire, it may be because it's new. Every fire takes time to spread.

One of the most difficult things to do in branding is to step out of your own shoes and into those of your customers and prospects. It's a critical first step in effectively conveying your message. If you can sustain your brand by preaching to the choir, go for it. But if you need to expand your customer base, recognize that what you do and how you think is not necessarily reflected in your target audience's behavior. Look, listen, and feel through their eyes, ears, and hands, and you might see more of their feet crossing your threshold.

CONCLUSION

TO BE CONTINUED

THE OXYMORONIC TITLE OF THIS FINAL CHAPTER IS MEANT SOME-what tongue in cheek. I trust by now you'll agree that there are no limits to effective branding. There is also no shortage of examples of companies using (or neglecting) its best practices. One of the things I love about what I do is that I get to observe and evaluate (and, in my company, work with) great brands as they advance the cause of branding excellence. There are always new stories that illuminate old principles, and occasionally my team will stumble on a principle that's been there all along but we hadn't yet realized.

My hope is that within the past couple of hundred pages you've done the same, finding not just one but many different ideas you can apply to your brand that perhaps you had yet to consider. One thing is certain: If more brands employed the principles of power branding, there would be many more powerful brands in the world.

Which takes us back to the beginning. It's hard to argue with the assertion that a brand is a company's most valuable asset, for the singular reason that its value need never decline. That said, there's no guarantee that any given brand will increase in value on a consistent basis. In fact, I daresay that's the exception rather than the rule. It's just plain hard to do good branding day after day, month after month, and year after year.

Power branding is not unlike getting in shape. Good intentions alone won't cut it. Sure, it's helpful to join a gym and develop a workout plan, and setting weight loss (or muscle gain) goals can be motivating. But nothing replaces, as Nike might put it, just doing it. You have to fight off the desire to roll over in bed on cold winter mornings and hoist yourself up, get to the gym, and work up a sweat day after day, until it becomes part of your lifestyle. You probably won't see significant results right away, so you must develop the discipline to stay with the program for some time. That's where most self-improvement initiatives—and branding programs—go awry.

Power branding is not an intention, nor is it merely an action. It's a commitment. That thought was driven home to me when I was sitting in a particularly frustrating meeting with the marketing team of a consumer brand that had done so much good work identifying their why, who, what, how, when, and where, with demonstrated positive early returns. But as we've seen, entropy is the universal principle that everything in the universe (including a well-designed branding program) tends toward disarray. That was what was unfolding before my eyes as the team members began rationalizing why so much of what they had intended to execute wasn't getting done.

So many things can derail a branding program. When a new CEO comes on board, he or she might change corporate strategy, potentially requiring a reexamination of brand strategy. Sometimes it's a new CMO who, rightly or wrongly, suffers from the not-invented-here syndrome. Sometimes the competitive landscape shifts, causing panic in the hallways of your company, leading to compromises (or worse, abandonment) of good branding principles. More often than not, it's the tyranny of the urgent that causes people to lose sight of what's important. And sometimes everyone involved (perhaps including you) just gets bored. That last one is particularly galling.

Never forget this maxim: In branding—as with everything else in business—strategy without execution is only theory. And effective execution takes time. It takes a while to seed a brand idea throughout all of the divisions, departments, systems, processes, and expressions of a company, and even more time for it to seep into the consciousness of employees, customers, and prospects. If you're not willing to invest the time in execution, don't waste the time in planning.

By contrast, show me a company that's consistently well aligned around a powerful idea, and I'll show you a company that's thriving. Branding and corporate culture are close cousins; the former is in many ways simply the expression of the latter. Healthy corporate cultures—those in which there is a great deal of top-to-bottom alignment around vision, mission, and value proposition—have a huge advantage in executing on a powerful brand proposition. Speaking as a practitioner, I've seen that it's much easier to rally the troops around a clear direction when they're all fighting for the same cause. I've also witnessed a lot of solid brand ideas die premature deaths due to internal sabotage. It's a tremendous waste of corporate (and human) capital.

I encourage you to take a deep breath and an honest look at your corporate culture. If it's not healthy, your biggest challenge may not be one of branding but of internal dynamics, and until you address them, nothing else matters. But here's the good news: A thoughtful, well-developed branding program can be a stake in the ground around which everyone can lock arms. Because a brand, properly defined, drives every aspect of the business, the development of a deliberate and thorough branding plan can right a lot of internal wrongs.

After that, it's all about the doing.

NOTES

INTRODUCTION

1. "Best Global Brands 2012," Interbrand, 2013, http://www.interbrand.com /en/best-global-brands/2012/Best-Global-Brands-2012-Brand-View.aspx# (accessed May 21, 2013).
2. "Top 100 Most Valuable Global Brands," Millward Brown, 2013, http://www .millwardbrown.com/BrandZ/Top_100_Global_Brands/Methodology.aspx (accessed May 23, 2013).
3. Ibid.
4. Will Rogers, "Quotable Quotes," Goodreads, http://www.goodreads.com /quotes/140216-it-takes-a-lifetime-to-build-a-good-reputation-but (accessed May 21, 2013).
5. "Mapping Your Global Reputation with 2013 Global RepTrak 100," Reputation Institute, March 2013, http://www.reputationinstitute.com/thought -leadership/global-reptrak-100 (accessed May 23, 2013).
6. "The CoreBrand Top 100 BrandPower Rankings," CoreBrand, 2012, http:// www.rankingthebrands.com/PDF/CoreBrand%20Brand%20Power%20 Ranking%202012,%20Corebrand.pdf (accessed May 20, 2013).
7. "Bestra's 2011 UK Reputation Dividend Ranking," Bestra Brand Consultants, March 31, 2011, http://www.bestrabrand.com/reports/Bestra_Reputation_Di vidend_letter.pdf (accessed May 20, 2013).
8. Larry Williams. "Internal Caterpillar speech," 1986.

CHAPTER 1: WHO COMES FIRST

1. "Flavor Fanatics," *Effie Worldwide,* 2012, http://www.effie.org/case_studies /case/2094 (accessed August 11, 2013).
2. John Zogby, *The Way We'll Be: The Zogby Report on the Transformation of the American Dream* (New York: Random House, 2008).

CHAPTER 2: SMALL MEANS BIG

1. John Sicher, "CSDs Declined for 7th Straight Year," *Beverage-Digest,* March 20, 2012, http://www.beverage-digest.com/pdf/top-10_2012.pdf (accessed May 20, 2013).
2. "Ferrari Focuses on Exclusivity," *Warc,* May 10, 2013, http://www.warc.com /LatestNews/News/Ferrari_focuses_on_exclusivity_.news?ID=31381 (accessed May 29, 2013).

CHAPTER 3: HAPPY ARE THE HUNTED

1. "Zappos.com: Happy People Making People Happy," *Effie Worldwide*, 2011, http://www.effie.org/case_studies/case/2035 (accessed May 28, 2013).

CHAPTER 4: UNCOMMON IS COMMON

1. Kimberly D. Williams, "Actually, Motel 6 Doesn't Leave the Light on for You," *Advertising Age*, August 30, 2007, http://adage.com/article/news/motel -6-leave-light/120172/ (accessed May 20, 2013).
2. R. W. Underhill, "Who's Minding the Brand?", *Arthur Andersen Retailing Is- sues Letter*, 11, no. 4 (July 1999): 1.
3. Williams, "Actually, Motel 6 Doesn't Leave the Light on for You."

CHAPTER 6: HEART BEATS WALLET

1. "Loyalty Programs Can Do More," *Warc*, May 23, 2013, http://www.warc .com/LatestNews/News/Loyalty_programs_can_do_more.news?ID=31436 (accessed May 29, 2013).

CHAPTER 8: IRRATIONAL IS RATIONAL

1. Joseph A. Mikels, Sam J. Maglio, Andrew E. Reed, and Lee J. Kaplowitz, "Should I Go with My Gut? Investigating the Benefits of Emotion-Focused Decision Making," *Emotion* 11 (August 2011): 743–753.
2. Alia J. Crum and Ellen J. Langer, "Mind-set Matters: Exercise and the Placebo Effect," *Psychological Science* 18 (2007): 165–171.
3. Jared Wadley, "Experiences Are Better When We Know They're about to End," U-M News Service, January 24, 2012, http://www.ns.umich.edu/new /releases/20177-experiences-are-better-when-we-know-theyre-about-to-end (accessed May 20, 2013).
4. Kathy Svitil, "Wine Study Shows Price Influences Perception," Caltech Media Relations, January 14, 2008, http://media.caltech.edu/press_releases/13091 (accessed May 20, 2013).
5. Gerd Gigerenzer, "Smart Heuristics: Gerd Gigerenzer," *Edge*, March 29, 2003, http://edge.org/conversation/smart-heuristics-gerd-gigerenzer (accessed May 21, 2013).
6. Ibid.

CHAPTER 9: CUSTOMERS AREN'T ALWAYS RIGHT

1. Steven Jobs, interview by David Sheff, *Playboy Interview: Steven Jobs*, February 1, 1985, http://www.redmondpie.com/steve-jobs-interview-in-playboy-1985/ (accessed August 8, 2013).
2. Steven P. Jobs interview, "Steve Jobs on Apple's Resurgence: 'Not a One- Man Show,'" May 12, 1998, http://www.businessweek.com/bwdaily/dnflash /may1998/nf80512d.htm (accessed August 8, 2013).
3. Adam Smith, *An Inquiry into the Nature & Causes of the Wealth of Nations, Vol 1* (London: Black, Tait, Longman, Rees, Orme, Brown and Green, 1776).

CHAPTER 10: RESEARCH CAN BE DECEIVING

1. Peter Sanders, "Just Asking . . . Andrew Stanton," *Wall Street Journal*, June 21, 2008, http://online.wsj.com/article/SB121400320722993395.html (accessed May 21, 2013).
2. Edward Taylor, "Toning Down the 'Bangle Butt,' BMW Redesigns Its 7 Series," *Wall Street Journal*, July 9, 2008, http://online.wsj.com/article/SB1 21555041646936817.html (accessed May 21, 2013).
3. Stephen Miller, "Snapple Guy's Overnight Success Took Decades," *Wall Street Journal*, May 23, 2013, http://online.wsj.com/article/SB10001424127887324 65940457849952427537419.html (accessed May 29, 2013).
4. Gary Hamel and C. K. Prahalad, "Seeing the Future First," *CNN Money*, September 5, 1994, http://money.cnn.com/magazines/fortune/fortune_arch ive/1994/09/05/79699/index.htm (accessed May 20, 2013).
5. Deborah Steinborn, "Talking about Design," *Wall Street Journal*, June 23, 2008, http://online.wsj.com/article/SB121372804603481659.html (accessed May 21, 3013).

CHAPTER 14: BRANDS 'R US

1. "Starbucks Demonstrates Unprecedented Level of Commitment to Partner (Employee) Coffee Education and Training," Starbucks, February 26, 2008, http://news.starbucks.com/article_print.cfm?article_id=69 (accessed May 23, 2013).
2. Ibid.

CHAPTER 15: YOUR BRAND IS THEIRS

1. "Netflix Officers & Directors," Netflix, 2012, http://ir.netflix.com/manage ment.cfm (accessed May 23, 2013).

CHAPTER 17: CONSENSUS IS GOOD

1. Steve McKee, *When Growth Stalls* (San Francisco: Jossey-Bass, 2009).
2. "You Have to See This: IBM's Jon Iwata 'Every Company Is a Publisher,'" *EC = MC: Every Company Is a Media Company*, September 27, 2010, http://www .everycompanyisamediacompany.com/every-company-is-a-media-/2010/09 /you-have-to-see-this-ibms-jon-iwata-every-company-is-a-publisher.html (accessed May 23, 2013).
3. Ibid.

CHAPTER 18: IDEAS ARE IT

1. "GE in Australia and New Zealand," GE Australia website, http://www .ge.com/au/company/factsheet_au.html (accessed August 11, 2013).
2. "Global R&D Fact Sheet," GE corporate website, http://www.ge.com/about -us/research/factsheet (accessed August 11, 2013).

CHAPTER 19: MARGINS TAKE MONEY

1. "How Share of Voice Wins Share of Market," *IPA*, July 29, 2009, http://www .ipa.co.uk/News/how-share-of-voice-wins-share-of-market (accessed May 23, 2013).

CHAPTER 20: RELEVANCE RULES

1. Ellen Byron, "Beauty, Prestige and Worry Lines," *Wall Street Journal,* August 20, 2007, http://onlinYe.wsj.com/article/SB118756615565702401.html (accessed May 28, 2013).
2. "History & Heritage: Revolution," General Motors, n.d., http://www.gm.com /company/historyAndHeritage/revolution.html (accessed May 23, 2013).
3. "History & Heritage: Rebirth," General Motors, n.d., http://www.gm.com /company/historyAndHeritage/rebirth.html (accessed May 23, 2013).
4. Mary Wells Lawrence, "Mary Wells Lawrence Quotes," *QuoteSea,* n.d., http:// www.quotesea.com/quotes/by/mary-wells-lawrence (accessed May 24, 2013).

CHAPTER 21: SIMPLICITY SELLS

1. Thomas Friedman, *The World Is Flat* (New York: Farrar, Straus and Giroux, 2005).
2. Jay Conrad Levinson, *Guerilla Advertising* (Boston: Houghton Mifflin Company, 1994), 134.
3. Volatire, "Voltaire Quotes," *Brainy Quote,* n.d., http://www.brainyquote.com /quotes/quotes/v/voltaire125632.html (accessed May 23, 2013).
4. "Subway Tops Brand Value Growth List," *Warc,* May 1, 2013, http://www .warc.com/LatestNews/News/Subway_tops_brand_value_growth_list_ .news?ID=31335 (accessed May 29, 2013).
5. Andy Reinhardt, "Steve Jobs: 'There's Sanity Returning,'" *Businessweek,* May 25, 1998, http://www.businessweek.com/1998/21/b3579165.htm (accessed May 25, 2013).
6. Warren Buffett, "Quotes About Simple," *GoodReads,* n.d., http://www.good reads.com/quotes/tag/simple (accessed May 24, 2013).

CHAPTER 23: DIFFERENT IS REFRESHING

1. "Morgan Freeman in a Commercial for Listerine," 22 Words, June 23, 2011, http://twentytwowords.com/2011/06/23/morgan-freeman-in-a-commercial -for-listerine-before-he-was-famous-1973/ (accessed May 23, 2013).
2. "Altoids: The Curiously Strong Mints," Wrigley, 2012, http://www.wrigley .com/global/brands/altoids.aspx (accessed May 23, 2013).
3. Alice Z. Cuneo, "Marketer of the Year: On Target," *Advertising Age,* December 11, 2000, http://adage.com/article/news/marketer-year-target/31878/ (accessed August 11, 2013).

CHAPTER 24: FEELINGS COME FIRST

1. "The DoubleTree by Hilton Cookie," Hilton, 2012, http://doubletree3.hilton .com/en/about/cookie.html (accessed May 23, 2013).

CHAPTER 26: COUNTERBRANDING WORKS

1. David Halloway, "The Annual Bowl of Puppies," *Animal Planet,* January 2013, http://animal.discovery.com/tv-shows/puppy-bowl/about-this-show/about -puppy-bowl.htm (accessed May 21, 2013).

2. "Menu & Nutrition," Carl Karcher Enterprises, Inc., 2013, http://www.carlsjr .com/menu/nutritional_calculator (accessed May 21, 2013).

CHAPTER 27: SCARCITY DRIVES VALUE

1. Semil Shah, "Why Are Diamonds So Expensive," Quora, March 6, 2011, http://www.quora.com/Diamonds/Why-are-diamonds-so-expensive (accessed May 21, 2013).

CHAPTER 29: INNOVATION PREVENTS LIQUIDATION

1. Brad Stone, "What's in Amazon's Box? Instant Gratification," *Bloomberg BusinessWeek,* November 24, 2010, http://www.businessweek.com/magazine/con tent/10_49/b4206039292096.htm#p1 (accessed May 24, 2013).
2. "Connectivity Brings New Opportunities," Warc, May 20, 2013, http://www .warc.com/LatestNews/News/Connectivity_brings_new_opportunities_ .news?ID=31415 (accessed May 29, 2013).

CHAPTER 31: FIRST IMPRESSIONS MATTER

1. "Are You a Busy, Single Professional? Try Pre-Dating Speed Dating Events!" Pre-Dating Speed Dating, 2013, http://www.pre-dating.com/ (accessed May 23, 2013).
2. Michael Sunnafrank, "Predicted Outcome Value in Initial Conversations," *Communication Research Reports* 5 (1988): 169–172.
3. Gitte Lindgaard et al., "Attention Web Designers: You Have 50 Milliseconds to Make a Good First Impression!" *Behaviour and Information Technology* 25 (2006): 115–126.
4. Steve McKee, "The Art of First Impressions," *Bloomberg BusinessWeek,* March 10, 2006, http://www.businessweek.com/stories/2006-03-10/the-art-of-first -impressionsbusinessweek-business-news-stock-market-and-financial-advice (accessed May 28, 2013).

CHAPTER 32: SLOGANS ARE OVERRATED

1. "Ad Age Advertising Century: Top 10 Slogans," *Advertising Age,* March 29, 1999, http://adage.com/article/special-report-the-advertising-century/ad-age -advertising-century-top-10-slogans/140156/ (accessed May 20, 2013).
2. "Best Global Brands 2012," Interbrand, 2013, http://www.interbrand.com/en /best-global-brands/2012/Best-Global-Brands-2012-Brand-View.aspx# (accessed May 21, 2013).
3. "McDonald's Unveils 'I'm Lovin' It' Worldwide Brand Campaign," McDonald's, September 2, 2003, http://mcdepk.com/imlovinit/downloads/ili_lead_re lease.pdf (accessed May 23, 2013).

CHAPTER 33: TESTING MAY FAIL

1. Jean Haliday, "GM Rethinks the Merits of Ad Pre-Testing," *Advertising Age,* April 23, 2001, http://adage.com/article/news/gm-rethinks-merits-ad-pre -testing/54955/ (accessed May 24, 2013).

2. "The Global Index of Creative Excellence in Advertising," *Gunn Report*, 2013, http://www.gunnreport.com (accessed May 23, 2013).
3. Marsha Lindsay, "Branding Revelations That Will Make You Rethink How You Define and Leverage Your Brand," Lindsay, Stone & Briggs, 2005, http://www.lsb.com/uploads/brandworks/branding.pdf (accessed May 24, 2013).
4. Robert B. Zajonc, "Mere Exposure: A Gateway to the Subliminal," *Current Directions in Psychological Science* 10 (December 2001): 224–228.
5. Bruce Tait, "How 'Marketing Science' Undermines Brands," *Admap*, October 2004, http://taitsubler.com/articles/how-marketing-science-undermines-brands (accessed May 24, 2013).
6. James Hurman, "The Case Against Pretesting," Y&R, n.d., http://www.yr.com/sites/vmldev.com/files/thinksaydo.pdf (accessed May 24, 2013).
7. Jon Steel, *Truth, Lies and Advertising: The Art of Account Planning* (New York: Wiley, 1998), 223–245.
8. Tait, "How 'Marketing Science' Undermines Brands."

CHAPTER 35: LESS IS OFTEN MORE

1. Christopher Helman, "Stand Up Brand," Forbes, July 9, 2001, http://www.forbes.com/forbes/2001/0709/127.html (accessed August 11, 2013).

CHAPTER 36: GAPS ARE GOOD

1. "Spark Plug Gap Settings," The Green Spark Plug Co. website, http://www.gsparkplug.com/shop/spark-plug-gap-settings (accessed August 7, 2013).
2. Ernest Hemmingway, "Death in the Afternoon," Goodreads, http://www.goodreads.com/work/quotes/360058-death-in-the-afternoon (accessed August 7, 2013).

CHAPTER 37: NOT ALL BELLS ARE EQUAL

1. "Consumer Marketing Initiatives," MasterCard Worldwide, 2013, http://www.mastercard.com/us/company/en/whatwedo/consumer_marketing.html (accessed May 23, 2013).

CHAPTER 38: PROMISES ARE PROBLEMATIC

1. Jonah Berger, "Arousal Increases Social Transmission of Information," *Psychological Science* 22 (April 2011): 891–893.

CHAPTER 39: CREATIVITY SELLS

1. Seth Stevenson, "The Most Interesting Man in the World," *Slate*, May 25, 2009, http://www.slate.com/articles/business/ad_report_card/2009/05/the_most_interesting_man_in_the_world.html (accessed May 25, 2013).
2. E. J. Schultz, "How This Man Made Dos Equis a Most Interesting Marketing Story," *Creativity Online*, March 5, 2012, http://creativity-online.com/news/the-story-behind-dos-equis-most-interesting-man-in-the-world/233112 (accessed May 20, 2013).

CHAPTER 41: BORING IS CRIMINAL

1. Mark Dolliver, "Consumers Don't Hate Ads," *Adweek,* July 16, 2009, http://www.adweek.com/news/advertising-branding/survey-consumers-dont-hate-ads-112896 (accessed August 7, 2013).

CHAPTER 42: HUMOR HELPS

1. "Tide to Go Super Bowl Ad Voted #1 in YouTube AdBlitz Contest," P&G, February 13, 2008, http://news.pg.com/press-release/pg-corporate-announcements/tide-gor-super-bowl-ad-voted-1-youtube-adblitz-contest (accessed May 28, 2013).
2. "Evian Roller Babies International Version," http://www.youtube.com/watch?v=XQcVllWpwGs.
3. Sharon Gaudin, "Oreo the Big Social Media Winner During Super Bowl," *Computerworld,* February 4, 2013, http://www.computerworld.com/s/article/9236493/Oreo_the_big_social_media_winner_during_Super_Bowl (accessed May 28, 2013).

CHAPTER 44: BEHAVIOR ISN'T BELIEF

1. "Gauge the Love in Your Loyalty Club: Facts & Stats," CMO Council, 2013, http://www.loyaltyleaders.org/facts.php?view=all (accessed May 23, 2013).
2. Liz Segal, Phil Auerbach, and Ido Segev, "The Power Points: Strategies for Making Loyalty Programs Work," McKinsey & Company, April 2013, http://csi.mckinsey.com/Home/Knowledge_by_topic/Marketing_and_sales/Power_of_points.aspx (accessed May 20, 2013).

CHAPTER 46: CONVERGENCE SPELLS OPPORTUNITY

1. "What's the Story?" MiniUSA, 2013, http://www.miniusa.com/faq.jsp?category=2#/contactFaq/faq/history-m (accessed May 23, 2013).
2. "MINI Brand History," Autoevolution, 2012, http://www.autoevolution.com/mini/history/ (accessed May 23, 2013).
3. Paul Williams, "Mini Cooper Ad Fires On All Cylinders," *Marketing Profs,* January 8, 2010, http://www.mpdailyfix.com/mini-cooper-ad-fires-on-all-cylinders/ (accessed May 23, 2013).

CHAPTER 49: SALES AND MARKETING MIX

1. "Burberry: Our Strategy," Burberry, 2013, http://www.burberryplc.com/about_burberry/our_strategy?WT.ac=Our+Strategy (accessed May 23, 2013).

CHAPTER 50: INTEGRATION IS POWER

1. "Haagen-Dazs Loves Honey Bees (Titanium Silver Lion Cannes 2009)," Limeshot Design, n.d., http://limeshot.com/2010/haagen-dazs-loves-honey-bees-titanium-silver-lion-cannes-2009 (accessed May 28, 2013).

CHAPTER 54: ANALOG IS AWESOME

1. Robert Bensen, "Top Ten Most Valuable Vinyl Records," DigitalDreamDoor. com, July 2009, http://www.digitaldreamdoor.com/pages/music-news/benson -Top-Valuable-Records.html (accessed May 20, 2013).
2. "These Audiophiles Prefer Vinyl to Digital," VinylFanatics.com, April 10, 2008, http://vinylfanatics.com/index.php/news-mainmenu-2/1-latest/299-th ese-audiophiles-prefer-vinyl-to-digital (accessed May 23, 2013).

CHAPTER 55: INVESTING RETURNS

1. Natalie Zmuda, "Dr Pepper Ups Marketing Spend, Readies for Growth," *AdvertisingAge*, May 4, 2009, http://adage.com/article/cmo-interviews/dr -pepper-ups-marketing-spending-readies-growth/136392/ (accessed May 21, 2013).
2. Paul Ziobro, "Dr Pepper Sees Sticky Prices Sweetening Profits," *Wall Street Journal*, December 28, 2010, http://online.wsj.com/article/SB100014240527 48703766704576009913684690594.html?KEYWORDS=Dr+Pepper+sees +sticky+prices (accessed May 21, 2013).

CHAPTER 56: ROI MAY BE DECEIVING

1. "The CoreBrand Top 100 BrandPower Rankings," CoreBrand, 2012, http:// www.rankingthebrands.com/PDF/CoreBrand%20Brand%20Power%20 Ranking%202012,%20Corebrand.pdf (accessed May 24, 2013).

CHAPTER 57: ACCRETION IS AMAZING

1. Lisa Lacy, "Kool-Aid Man Makeover Stirs Up Digital Content," ClickZ, April 17, 2013, http://www.clickz.com/clickz/news/2261640/koolaid-man -makeover-stirs-up-digital-content (accessed May 20, 2013).

CHAPTER 58: PATIENCE IS A VIRTUE

1. Associated Press, "TV Guide Names Top 50 Shows," CBS News, February 11, 2009, http://www.cbsnews.com/2100-207_162-507388.html (accessed August 7, 2013).

CHAPTER 59: VISIBILITY BRINGS CREDIBILITY

1. James Surowiecki, interview on *The Wisdom of Crowds* website, *Q&A with James Surowiecki*, undated (accessed August 8, 2013).

CHAPTER 61: IT'S OK TO BE UNCOMFORTABLE

1. Bob Garfield, "We Have Located the Monkeys," *Advertising Age*, February 24, 2007, http://adage.com/article/garfield-the-blog/located-monkeys/1151 33/ (accessed May 24, 2013).

CHAPTER 62: ENTROPY HAPPENS

1. Nanette Byrnes, "Burger King's Big Misstep," *BusinessWeek*, May 14, 2009, http://www.businessweek.com/magazine/content/09_21/b4132050825864 .htm (accessed May 20, 2013).

2. Erin Dostal, "What's Ahead for New Burger King CEO," *Nation's Restaurant News,* April 12, 2013, http://nrn.com/latest-headlines/whats-ahead-new-burger-king-ceo (accessed May 20, 2013).

CHAPTER 63: SIZE WON'T SAVE YOU

1. Louis Llovio, "Former Circuit City CEO and Chairman Talks of Company's Demise," TimesDispatch.com, January 16, 2013, http://www.timesdispatch.com/business/former-circuit-city-ceo-and-chairman-talks-of-company-s/article_8e219f23-721b-5a54-b6c2-3e1b35536557.html (accessed May 20, 2013).
2. Ibid.
3. Anita Hamilton, "Why Circuit City Busted, While Best Buy Boomed," *TIME,* November 11, 2008, http://www.time.com/time/business/article/0,8599,1858079,00.html (accessed May 20, 2013).

CHAPTER 66: DOING GOOD MIGHT HURT

1. Valerie Bauerlein, "Pepsi Hits 'Refresh' on Donor Project," *Wall Street Journal,* January 30, 2011, http://online.wsj.com/article/SB10001424052748704832704576114171399171138.html (accessed May 21, 2013).
2. Ibid.
3. Ibid.

CHAPTER 67: TACTICS ARE DECEIVING

1. Amy Bryer, "Quizno's [*sic*] Spokes-Rats Grab Attention," *Denver Business Journal,* April 25, 2004, http://www.bizjournals.com/denver/stories/2004/04/26/story7.html?page=all (accessed May 24, 2013).
2. "Quizno's [*sic*]," *YouTube,* March 31, 2006, http://www.youtube.com/watch?v=aZrks-BPeLQ (accessed May 24, 2013).

CHAPTER 69: FOCUS CAN BE FLEETING

1. Connie Madon, "Walmart Cuts Prices to 'Increase Customer Excitement,'" *Blogging Stocks,* April 10, 2010, http://www.bloggingstocks.com/2010/04/10/walmart-cuts-prices-to-fend-off-sluggish-sales/ (accessed August 7, 2013).

CHAPTER 70: ASPIRATIONS MAY BACKFIRE

1. "Wells Fargo: Our Values," Wells Fargo, 2013, https://www.wellsfargo.com/invest_relations/vision_values/4 (accessed May 23, 2013).

CHAPTER 71: CELEBRITIES BITE

1. "Accenture Cuts Woods as Sponsor," ESPN, December 14, 2009, http://espn.go.com/blog/sportscenter/post/_/id/10333/accenture-drops-woods-as-sponsor http://sports.espn.go.com/golf/news/story?id=4739219m (accessed May 20, 2013).

CHAPTER 74: SPEED CAN KILL

1. Lauren Coleman-Lochner and Adam Satariano, "Penney Nabbing Johnson from Apple Sets 'Huge Expectation,'" Bloomberg News, June 15, 2011, http://

www.bloomberg.com/apps/news?pid=2065100&sid=aMIKEDh1YwC8 (accessed May 20, 2013).

2. Ibid.
3. Phil Wahba, "Penney Sales Tumble Again, Amid Hopeful Signs," Reuters, May 7, 2013, http://www.reuters.com/article/2013/05/07/us-jcpenney-results-idUSBRE94615K20130507 (accessed May 20, 2013).

INDEX